FOL
4—

# Words in Place

*Reconnecting with Nature through Creative Writing*

## Paul Matthews

Hawthorn Press

Published by Hawthorn Press, Hawthorn House, 1 Lansdown Lane, Stroud,
Gloucestershire, GL5 1BJ, UK
Tel: (01453) 757040 Fax: (01453) 751138
info@hawthornpress.com
www.hawthornpress.com
Cover illustration by Ray Hedger
Illustrations © Margaret Shillan
Author photograph by Tatjana Zuboff
Cover design by Hawthorn Press, Stroud, Gloucestershire
Design and typesetting by Lynda Smith at Hawthorn Press, Stroud, Gloucestershire
Printed and bound in England by Antony Rowe Ltd, Chippenham, Wiltshire

Margaret Shillan has worked for many years at Emerson College as an artist, painting
teacher and teacher trainer
'Portrait of Ashdown Forest' copyright ©Roger Penn, 1984, first published by Robert
Hale Ltd. Map of Emerson College reproduced by kind permission of Emerson College.
Credit: *Primavera*, c.1478, (tempera on panel) by Botticelli, Sandro (1444/5-1510)
©Galleria degli Uffizi, Florence, Italy/The Bridgeman Art Library. Nationality/copyright
status: Italian/out of copyright. *An Experiment on a Bird in the Air Pump* by Joseph Wright
of Derby reproduced by kind permission of The National Gallery, London. 'Golden Lines'
by Gerard de Nerval, trans. by Robert Duncan from *Bending the Bow*, copyright ©1968
by Robert Duncan, reprinted by permission of New Directions Publishing Corporation.
The poems by children on pages 48 and 213 are reprinted here by kind permission of
Richard Lewis, director of Touchstone Center for Children, New York. They first
appeared in *Miracles*, edited by Richard Lewis, published by Simon and Schuster, 1966.
The poem on page 213 was originally titled 'My Brain'.
I am grateful to those of my students who have granted permission to include their
writings and trust that those I have not been able to trace are happy to be included.
Every effort has been made to trace the ownership of all copyrighted material. If any
omission has been made, please bring this to the publisher's attention so that proper
acknowledgement may be given in future editions.
British Library Cataloguing in Publication Data applied for

ISBN 978-1-903458-69-3

# Contents

## Opening our Senses to Each Other and the World . . . 24

*from direct observation of whatever we encounter, lead into a consideration of what imagination is, and the suggestion that it is closely linked to the development of our sense perception. We explore ways in writing to discover afresh the purity and clarity of seeing which we possessed in childhood. We end with the question of how close up to nature we can get through language.*

WEEK TWO

# Earth, Water, Air and Fire

*We turn our attention to the four elements, Earth, Water, Air and Fire, and to how they manifest in our surroundings. Direct observation and memories of encounters with these elements are taken as a basis for writing. The elements are, however, more than states of matter. As qualities they can be found both in the many gestures of the natural world and in human temperament. Furthermore, their dynamics are observable in how we move, speak and write. These we practise here, asking how each element in turn can lend its quality to our writing. We close with a diagram in which these four qualities are shown to stand as an imaginative gateway between inner and outer worlds.*

WEEK THREE

# Turning a New Leaf

*Having explored the four elements as qualities of movement and language, we now extend this into modes of encountering the world of plants, concentrating first upon the mode of Earth (the most detached and formed), and of Water (in which we attend to movement and relationship). In grammar these manifest as statement and question. The writing that arises may seem to lack poetry at first, but if our words are to have truth in them as well as beauty then this more scientific mode provides a necessary ground and discipline for the imagination.*

WEEK FOUR

## The Flowering Garden and Our Responses to it ... 111

*Now that we have faithfully engaged in these modes of Earth and Water we can turn with confidence towards what Air and Fire invite us into. In language they manifest as exclamation and command, and in the I/You relationship which gives more scope for imagination and poetry. Through exercises in moving, drawing and writing the language of nature begins to reveal itself.*

WEEK FIVE

## The Animals in Nature . . . . . . . . . . . . . . . . . . . . . . 134

*We begin to engage with the animal kingdom, starting once again in observational mode and with remembered encounters. It soon becomes clear that the shift from plant to animal naturally animates the story-maker in us. Animals like to play, especially when young, and this gives us permission to be playful with our words in response to them, characterising what is essential rather than coldly defining them. In general the writing exercises suggested here start with the I/It mode referred to earlier, and then invite us to be open to the possibility of meeting I to You.*

WEEK SIX

# Giving Voice to the Animals

*The verb nature of the animals invites us to lend them our words so that they, too, may find a voice through riddle, prayer and fable. This is the third stage (I/I) of the process that we practised earlier. The work that we began with story-making is taken further into the creation of origin stories.*

WEEK SEVEN

# Being Human

*Our progress through the realms of nature brings us now to a consideration of what it means to be human. An imagination of the human being in respectful companionship with stone, plant and beast is presented. The seasonal Whitsun festival gives us the opportunity to develop our thoughts on imagination and human creativity as we explore, through written conversation and the writing of letters, how language finds its deepest destiny as a means of communion between people. We arrive at a turning point in which 'heart work' takes forward the 'work of eyes'.*

WEEK EIGHT

# The Story We Belong To

*The study of a Grimm's fairy tale takes us more deeply now into realms of soul where the objects and creatures of the outer world serve as a language for our human inwardness, and the energy of the narrative becomes rhythmically patterned. In this context the practice of writing fictional letters is taken further. We then take up the task of writing our own soul story. A series of exercises in which the common matter of our biographies is transformed through fantasy, dream and play lead us towards the possibility of making up a story that is at the same time true. The question of how imagination can serve the truth naturally comes back again.*

# Preface in the Form of a Letter

You have kindly invited me to write a preface for your new book and it is a pleasure to do so. I hope you do not mind me writing it as a personal letter; in that way I may be able to find the voice I need to meet and greet your work.

As you know I have been informally associated with Emerson College for many years and have come to admire what it represents. I have many memories of the college but one of my earliest and strongest is of sitting in one of the dining rooms in Pixton House and being strangely moved by the wild flowers set out on every table. Such a small thing! Yet it told me so much about the place I was visiting: that it cared about nature, that it cherished beauty, that it had a precise eye for detail, and valued intimacy and spontaneity. My subsequent visits confirmed and deepened this early impression. And, as the years passed, so I began to see that Emerson College represented a rare experiment in England to keep the nouns of *education* and *life* in the closest possible contact, to conceive education as the richest amplification of all the potential that lay dormant in life itself. An invaluable experiment that stands in need of greater recognition.

Your book is on Creative Writing but the kind of approach you espouse is so much more than another pragmatic course in this now popular field. I began my thoughts with Emerson College because I believe it has been the crucial matrix for your own approach to the teaching of writing. If you had been working in, shall we say, a modern university, your course could not have evolved to its present level. The institution would have choked the sprouting plant. Your personal and intuitive notions needed the rich soil of Emerson: they required the open landscape, the particular individuals, the cultural history and the generous ethos of the college. Somehow, it is as if the *genius loci* has found a further expression in the articulation of your writing programme.

And what I admire in your work, particularly, are three interrelated principles: that the word – whether written or spoken – is a living energy, that poetry is an imaginative discipline and that Creative Writing enhances subtle acts of healing. I have witnessed these principles in action at Emerson, particularly in your Summer School, *Poetry OtherWise*, and seen how they can transform people's lives. My own experience of teaching and writing tells me these axioms are true and seminal; but I am also sure, generally, that the latter principle is the one most neglected. The emphasis you place on being and belonging (and *coming to be* and *coming to belong* within a creative universe) is so very important. It has profound implications for both the understanding of community and the deep meaning of ecology. The principle gleams from your pages, a fierce light in the collective dark.

Yet what you offer here is not, of course, an abstract treatise but a living manual based on years of considered experience. It seems to me you offer a course not only in the sense of a coherent educational programme but, also, in the sense of a route to be taken, a path which opens out into an ever larger cosmos. For me, the warm guardian spirit of Ralph Waldo Emerson hovers over the entire script, making the journey possible, making it memorable. I am sure that everyone committed to the art of education, in the broadest sense, will find inspiration in what you have written, as will, most especially, those drawn to both the arts of writing and healing.

I wish the book well.

*Peter Abbs, Professor of Creative Writing*
*at the University of Sussex, Summer 2006*

*I dedicate this book to all my students over the years,*

*thanking them for helping me learn what I have to teach.*

PM

# About the Author

Paul Matthews teaches at Emerson College, in Forest Row, East Sussex, UK. His early explorations into the nature of language and the teaching of Creative Writing were published in *Sing Me the Creation* (Hawthorn Press, 1994). In the present volume he turns his attention to the language of nature, seeking to open within the human heart an eye for our mineral, plant and animal companions. Emerson College and its beautiful surroundings are taken as the model for a work which writers, teachers, group leaders, therapists, and nature lovers will find useful and inspiring whatever their environment.

# The Way In

This is the door to Emerson College, an educational and cultural community that draws particular inspiration from the insights of Rudolf Steiner. For many years, first as student, then as lecturer and resident poet, I have walked through this door or lingered outside it talking with friends and colleagues, and as I come now to share the work that I have done I find it impossible to abstract my words from the place and people that have given them context.

1

For this reason, rather than writing the usual Creative Writing handbook, I have structured this book around a nine-week full-time course, *Working with Imagination*, that I developed here over several spring times. I make on-going reference to 'the group' that I am working with, but actually this is somewhat fictionalised as I have conflated many groups into one group, drawing upon my own experiments and collaborations over those years, and including writings produced by some of those with whom it has been my joy to work. I also address myself directly to you, the reader, inviting you to pick up your pen and join us in the venture.

## How the book is shaped

The shape of the book is basically a progress through the different realms of nature – from mineral to plant to animal to human. My ordering of the themes into 'Weeks' rather than 'Chapters' arises out of a desire to include an attention to 'words in time' alongside the emphasis on 'place' implied by the book's title. If I take April to June as my model, this does not mean you should feel bound to any particular season for the work. Generally, each 'Week' starts with the immediate observation and naming of what the world presents, and then moves towards a closer imaginative engagement, seeking out the essences and archetypes hidden within the manifold gestures of nature. Just as the tree in its quickening moves through lawful yet ever-surprising stages of growth and metamorphosis, so I hope you will experience an organic unfolding in the turning of these pages. In the end, though, it is up to you to pick and choose exercises, or whole sections, best suited to your own creative purposes. As individual writer, poet, teacher, therapist, environmentalist, or self-help group, you should feel free to adapt it to your own needs, culture and environment.

# *Who is the book for?*

- **Creative Writing groups.** As mentioned already, the work (in the first instance) proposes a group of people coming together with the common aim of supporting and challenging each other in the art and craft of writing, and in schooling the faculty of imagination. If you do choose to form such a group everything will depend upon the interest and attention that you give to one other. It may seem, at first, like a random bunch of people sitting on their separate chairs. Potentially, however, it is a circle of fire, an active open space waiting to receive a grace in words that no one working alone, perhaps, could quite reach up to. In my own experience this is best fostered through a playful and collaborative working with words, enlivening the use of image, rhythm and rhyming, before moving into more individual projects. If you are the group leader it will be your responsibility, initially, to nurture this. If you are working without a designated leader then you will all have to carry that awareness. Those hoping for commercial success through writing are unlikely to be satisfied by the kind of group dynamics proposed in this book. I do, when invited, give strong or challenging advice on the craft of writing. In general, though, I seek to establish a working ethos in which everyone, in their own time, can find the courage to uncover their unique and authentic voice. Be sure to celebrate that voice in the group whenever it makes its appearance. Written voice. Spoken voice. I encourage people to read out what they have written, in small groups, then in the larger circle, and to find ways of giving helpful feedback. It is by no means easy to get this right, and you will have to be merciful with each other if you sometimes fail to do so. Silence, of course, needs to be respected.

- **The individual writer.** Although the format of the book assumes a group context, writers working alone with a serious intent to develop their craft and creativity will have little difficulty in transforming the exercises accordingly (these are marked with an X, numbered, and printed in bold, to be followed easily as stepping stones through the general flood). There are excellent books on Creative Writing (classically, *Writing Down the Bones* by Natalie Goldberg[1]) that indicate ways of tapping those inner sources of feeling which ultimately give substance to our words. My own way, of turning attention outwards to stones and cabbages and tigers, is a complement not contradiction to that approach, for you will soon find that such everyday things, devotedly attended to, begin to interpret and become a language for what lives most deeply inside you. It would be good to commit yourself to a time each day when the writing takes precedence over everything else. Even if you sit, pen in hand, and write nothing, it signals to your creative mind that you are ready and waiting. There is no denying that the craft of writing can be a lonely pursuit. I suggest, therefore, that once in a while you find a trusted and discerning friend with whom to share the results of your work. Language lives between people; it needs to be tested upon the world.

- **Teachers of children.** This work of bringing language alive in groups began for me when, as a teacher of children in Steiner/Waldorf Schools, I was determined to find a way in which the study of literature could be combined with the creation of it. My recent work has been with adults, yet the urgency of this concern is never far away. Children come into this world expecting to meet a lively and imaginative use of language in those who teach them. If they do not then their own natural gifts for language may remain unnurtured. Often in my attempts to foster creativity I draw upon childhood sources, many of which have found their way into these pages – texts readily available for use in the classroom. As for the exercises presented here, if you find the right context children are sure to take delight in them, developing confidence in their craft and creative abilities as they do so. Some days, in search of inspiration, you might simply want to open the book and put your finger down at random. You will also find plenty of ideas for sustained projects in writing, particularly in relation to local geography and to the creatures of nature that are so dear to children's hearts.

- **Therapists, social workers, consultants, facilitators** and all whose task it is to serve the wellbeing of individuals and communities. Wendell Berry (in his book, *Standing by Words*[2]) draws a parallel between disintegration of both personality and community that has taken place over the last 150 years, and the current disintegration of language. In support of this he diagnoses two diseases of language – one in which the world is absent but the speaker is present, the other where the world is present but the speaker is absent. Therapists in their consulting rooms will no doubt be familiar with individuals who suffer from the first, wrapped in a private language that has little reference to the world. And the social worker will know only too well the soul-less jargon of officialdom, and the consequences of mechanised social and educational structures that fail to address our human inwardness. Wendell Berry's contention that these disintegrations of personality and community will find healing only when we learn to 'stand by our words' (world and speaker both present in the act of language) provides a further context for the exercises offered here, intended as they are to help mend the rift between inner and outer experience. Some of my poetic companions (Jay Ramsay, and others) have had connections to *Lapidus*,[3] a group dedicated to poetry as a healing art, and I have worked with

'Survivors' groups in which people find renewed meaning in their lives through being creative together in writing. The playful and collaborative aspects of the book might prove particularly relevant in this regard, as indeed they would in any work or social situation in need of an enlivening activity.

- **Environmentalists.** Berry could have included the disintegration of our environment in the same context. The Book of Nature is more than metaphor ('book' and 'beech' spring from the same root) and if, caught in mechanistic thinking, we forget how to read the life-giving spirit that breathes between its lines and letters then meaning is lost and, at the hands of the agro-industry, the binding falls apart. Shakespeare knew all about 'books in the running brooks, sermons in stones',[4] of course, but Wendell Berry is one among a growing number of poets reawakening to this relationship between word and world. Peter Abbs (poetry editor of *Resurgence*) speaks powerfully in his anthology, *Earth Songs*,[5] for an emerging eco-poetics. And there are scientists such as Craig Holdredge, founder of the *Nature Institute*, who see the world in almost poetic terms. At the beginning of his book, *The Flexible Giant* (the subtitle of which is *Seeing the Elephant Whole*), Holdredge gathers together all the elephant's characteristics and then says:

> To keep analysis from taking on a life of its own, we can, while gaining knowledge of detail, continually return to the question, Who are you, elephant? The idea of the coherent organism, framed as a question, becomes the guiding light of inquiry.[6]

He ends the passage by saying: 'The challenge is to articulate that unity' – bringing to mind the story of those men who, washing an elephant in the dark, could only define it according to the bit they were assigned to. Such a coming together of poets and scientists for the encouragement and education of holistic awareness has been an important inspiration for me in writing *Words in Place*.

## Pen and paper

Whoever you are, and whether you are working alone or with companions, you will need a pen and a piece of paper. A pen is… a small machine for making marks with, I suppose; except that one morning you might catch yourself holding it poised in the air before you write. Then what would you call it? Something is stirring there, and the paper provides the matter on which to make the patterns of that movement visible. I am not sure, then, that all those ruled lines and margins are very helpful. A blank page will do – it allows the word-energy to come in from all directions, and even to take the form of drawings and doodlings if it wants to. Find yourself a notebook in which to gather the pieces that you have done. A finished book of work, handwritten, with sketches alongside, is always satisfying.

## Supporting activities

Any course that professes to be 'working with imagination' would do well to include drawing and painting, and some work with speech, singing and movement as supporting activities. Though it has not been possible to integrate these fully into the text, I do seriously contend that the life of language can be considerably enhanced through those less sedentary pursuits, and you will find suggestions for this among my many 'spells'. I am most grateful to my friend and colleague, Margaret Shillan, who in her sketches has tried to catch and bring alive the elusive spirit of the house, garden and surrounding countryside in which these words find their place. Hopefully this focus on a particular locality will give no cause for you to feel excluded. Read the whole thing as a fiction, if you will. Take it as a model and invitation to do something similar for the place (whether in town or countryside) in which your own words are grounded.

## Notes

[1] Goldberg, N., *Writing Down the Bones*, Shambala, 1986

[2] Berry, W., *Standing by Words*, North Point Press, 1983, p.24

[3] Lapidus can be contacted at BM LAPIDUS, London, WC1N 3XX

[4] Shakespeare, W., *As You Like It*, Act II, Scene I, Signet Classics, 1963, p.59

[5] Abbs, P., (ed.) *Earth Songs*, Green Books, 2002

[6] Holdredge, C., *The Flexible Giant*, The Nature Institute, 2003, p.3

# Falling into Place

Emerson College sits on a green Sussex hillside overlooking the village of Forest Row. On the far side of the valley, rising to a ridge of the Weald (the 'Wild'), is the Ashdown Forest, last remnant of the ancient forest of Anderida that (before farmers and ship-builders had their way) once stretched to the chalk cliffs of the south coast thirty miles away. Dense and difficult to penetrate, this was the last region of England to be converted to Christianity. When finally St. Dunstan and other Saxon missionaries did succeed, the county became so known for its godliness that it was called 'Silly (meaning 'holy') Sussex'. Many centuries later much of what now remains as the Ashdown Forest was declared a royal hunting park – hence

'Forest Row' (*Foret du Roi*, according to some), local place names such as Coleman's Hatch and Chelwood Gate indicating ways in to the forest through what at that time was the surrounding Pale. In 1929, at Kidbrooke Park (now the site of the local Steiner School), a pageant was held in celebration of the *Spirit of Anderida*.[1] That spirit was represented by the Hon. Mrs. Tatham riding on a white horse, her accompanying elves, gnomes and fairies being played by the children of Forest Row. Mr. Rudyard Kipling (by then resident in Sussex) was an honoured guest at the occasion.

## The literary environment

William Cobbett, author of *Rural Rides*,[2] and writing before the Romantic poets had opened eyes to the beauty of wilderness, spoke of Ashdown 'as verily the most villainously ugly spot I ever saw in England'. In more recent times, however, the Forest has been remapped for the imagination inside the front cover of *Winnie the Pooh*. A.A. Milne (the author of that well loved scripture) lived in nearby Hartfield, and you can find a memorial to him and to his illustrator, E.H. Shepherd, on top of the Forest at Gill's Lap (or 'Galleon's Lap', as it is called in *The House at Pooh Corner*). This is not just barren heathland, then, but is (with bits of golf-course interspersed) the 'enchanted place' where Christopher Robin, in saying goodbye to Pooh Bear, bade farewell to his childhood. Go stand above the Ha-Ha at the bottom of the Emerson College garden and you will see it, a dark clump of pine trees high on the ridge.

Sometimes, come to the end of study, I take my students up there and show them E.H. Shepherd's delightful drawing of the place, and read Milne's description of:

> ... sixty-something trees in a circle; and Christopher Robin
> knew it was enchanted because nobody had ever been able to

count whether it was sixty-three or sixty-four, not even when he tied a piece of string round each tree after he had counted it. Being enchanted, its floor was not like the floor of the Forest, gorse and bracken and heather, but close-set grass, quiet and smooth and green. It was the only place in the Forest where you could sit down carelessly, without getting up again almost at once and looking for somewhere else. Sitting there they could see the whole world spread out until it reached the sky, and whatever there was all the world over was with them in Galleon's Lap.[3]

On the next page is a map of the Ashdown Forest,[4] showing the names of its medieval Gates and Hatches. It pleases me to note the rough-hewn heart shape of its ancient boundary, and in my imagination I am colouring it green and filling it with all the rocks and streams and storms and trees and creatures that I have loved during my time of living here. At some point in our work together I suggest you make a hand-drawn map of your own local area, naming its outer details, but also depicting those places where important things have happened for you, or where local writers and artists have, through their words and imaginations, opened a heartscape for you beyond the usual boundaries of the senses. This map, for example, includes some of the places where the creator of Winnie the Pooh touched it with his words. A place becomes more real through being imagined.

But there are other musings woven into this landscape. St. Swithun's Church in nearby East Grinstead was the place of work and burial of Canon John Mason Neale who composed the famous Christmas carol 'Good King Wenceslas';[5] the line about the poor man gathering winter fuel 'right against the forest fence' grows in significance once you know the local context. Fifteen miles east is 'Penshurst' where, in the 16th century, Sir Phillip Sidney had his family seat and which, according to his companion

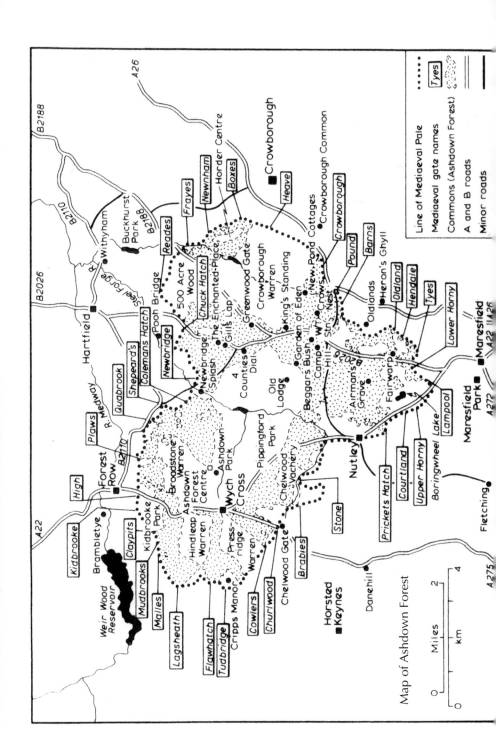

Map of Ashdown Forest

Line of Mediaeval Pale ┈┈┈
Mediaeval gate names
Commons (Ashdown Forest)
A and B roads
Minor roads

Tyes

Miles 0 2 4
km 0

Weir Wood Reservoir
Kidbrooke
Brambletye
Claypits
Mudbrooks
Kidbrooke Park
Malles
Lagsheath
Flawhatch
Tudbridge
Cripps Manor
Cowlers
Churlwood
Chelwood Gate
Brabies
Stone
Hindleap Warren
Broadstone Warren
Ashdown Forest Centre
Pressridge Warren
Ashdown Park
Wych Cross
Chelwood Vachery
Pippingford Park
Old Lodge
4 Counties Dial
Newbridge Splash
Newbridge
Pooh Bridge
500 Acre Wood
Chuck Hatch
The Enchanted Place
Gills Lap
Greenwood Gate
King's Standing
Crowborough Warren
Garden of Eden
Beggars Bush
Camp Hill
Airman's Grove
Fairwarp
Nutley
Prickets Hatch
Courtland
Upper Horny
Boringwheel Lake
Lampool
Lower Horny
Tyes
Hendale
Oldland
Heron's Ghyll
Oldlands
Barns
Pound
Crowborough
Heave
Crowborough Common
New Pond Cottages
Crow Sta.
W.T. Crowborough
Boxes
Newnham
Horder Centre
Frayes
Reades
Colemans Hatch
Sheppard's
Quabrook
Plaws
Forest Row
High
Steel Forge
Withyham
Buckhurst Park
Hartfield
R. Medway
Maresfield
Maresfield Park
Horsted Keynes
Danehill
Fletching

B2188
B2026
B2110
A26
A22
B2110
A272
A275
A22 //A26

in poetry, Ben Jonson, is no mere building, but truly a dwelling place.[6] A similar distance to the south, Virginia Woolf, yearning for a room of her own,[7] had one built for herself in her garden at 'Monk's House' in Rodmell, just the other side of Lewes. You can see it today, between two trees – a sweet chestnut close to the doorway, a horse chestnut leaning over the wall from the neighbouring graveyard. It was there that she filled her pockets with stones and crossed the fields to end her life in the river.

St. Swithun's Church, East Grinstead

# *Stone Cottage*

Stone Cottage

Most important for me has been the fact that, for three winters around the start of the First World War, the great Irish poet W.B. Yeats and the young American poet Ezra Pound were living and writing two miles up the road in 'Stone Cottage' in the village of Coleman's Hatch. Yeats would show Pound the poems that he was working on, and Pound who, with the pride of youth, assumed the task of helping Yeats forge a voice fit for the 20th century, would hand them back with 'piffle' and suchlike, scribbled in the margins. In a passage from *The Cantos* Pound describes a noise of wind in the chimney which was really 'Uncle William' composing aloud downstairs, distracting him from his own work in the room above 'at Stone Cottage in Sussex by the Waste Moor'.[8]

Ezra Pound, then in the process of creating his influential Imagist Movement (see p.45), wrote letters addressed from Coleman's Hatch outlining his emerging modernist doctrines:

Rhythm must have meaning... Language is made out of concrete things. General expressions in non-concrete terms are a laziness.[9]

Yeats bore this somewhat dictatorial tone with patience, writing later in the introduction to *A Vision* of:

Ezra Pound, whose art is the opposite of mine, whose criticism commends what I most condemn, a man with whom I should quarrel more than with anyone else if we were not united by affection...[10]

In that same introduction Yeats, acknowledging his wife's access to inspirational sources, writes 'When the automatic writing began we were staying in a hotel on the edge of the Ashdown Forest'[11] – the Ashdown Forest Hotel, in fact, in Forest Row, where he and Georgie spent the first days of their honeymoon in 1917. It just happens to be a few hundred yards from where I now live, except that it has been knocked down recently and replaced by a large apartment building. I have my doubts about automatic writing as a trustworthy source, yet when I walk past that spot each morning on my way to work I am happy to know that this small corner of the universe is open to the possibility of vision and its embodiment in great poetry, drama and story. In times of doubt I invoke the blessing of these two poets on my work; and in moments of boldness I thank them for preparing the ground for this labour of language that I am undertaking.

## Emerson College

Emerson College, founded by Francis Edmunds in 1962, moved to its present home on Pixton Hill in the summer of 1967, acquiring the neighbouring Tablehurst Farm the following year. I

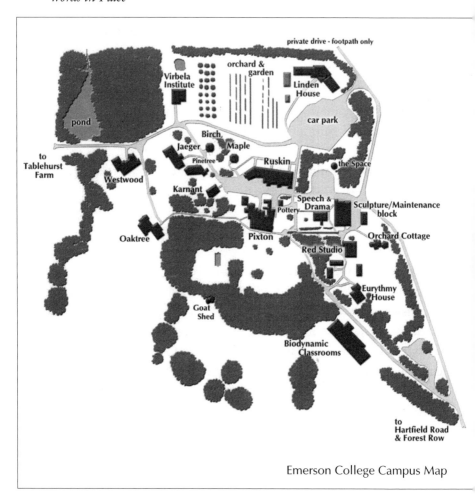

private drive - footpath only

orchard &
garden

Virbela
Institute

Linden
House

car park

pond

to
Tablehurst
Farm

Birch

Jaeger        Maple

Pinetree

Ruskin

the Space

Westwood

Karnant

Speech &
Pottery   Drama        Sculpture/Maintenance
                        block

Oaktree

Pixton                  Orchard Cottage

Red Studio

Eurythmy
House

Goat
Shed

Biodynamic
Classrooms

to
Hartfield Road
& Forest Row

Emerson College Campus Map

remember the occasion when my companions and I (I was a student then) walked with 'Mr. Edmunds' over the farm to claim it. The fire in his eye that morning confirmed for me that this indeed was what I had long longed for – a place of education which welcomed passionate concern into the learning process. Here, established just in time to catch a generation of potential 'drop-outs' from the system, was a college founded upon 'Rudolf Steiner's Image of Man'; not 'anti-university', as the fashion was in the 1960s, but 'pro-human' as Francis insisted. An idealistic time it was, for sure, but the 'community of works' that he envisioned then has continued to mature and grow, both here at Emerson College and in the neighbourhood. With its strong impulse for the renewing of culture and community, it can stand confidently alongside other experiments in adult education (Dartington, Findhorn, and the earlier Black Mountain College in North Carolina come to mind); and now, after more than forty years' work, it merits wider recognition.

## Rudolf Steiner

Rudolf Steiner (1861–1925) is many things to many people – Austrian philosopher, scientist, seer, architect, founder of biodynamic agriculture and Waldorf education... even 'bad but influential water colourist', as I once saw him described in a book on painting technique. He would have called himself a spiritual scientist, I suppose, gifted as he was with a subtlety of perception not granted to everyone, and yet intent on investigating and recording his spiritual insights with a modern scientific consciousness.

I first heard of him when I chanced upon a second-hand copy of one of his books, with Edelweiss pressed lovingly between the pages, and wrote a critique on it for my English teacher entitled 'Re-embodiment and Destiny'. A few days later I received it back with a note saying, 'I refuse to read this, but it looks well written'. Silly doctrines. Well worth studying further, I decided.

His detailed understanding that we are beings of body, soul and spirit with a creative destiny over many lifetimes (the thing which terrified my teacher) was immediately recognisable to me. What a relief it was on my arrival at Emerson College to discover, after years of self-doubt during my intellectual studies, a place of learning where this fuller picture of the human being was being lived and where my poetic notions, so foolish in the world's eyes, could be valued as having potential in my own training to become a teacher of children. When such doubts return (as they sometimes do) I take heart from Winnie the Pooh's famous dictum: 'Rabbit has brains. That's why he doesn't understand anything'.[12] In those stories it is only when Rabbit stops his busy intellectual chatter that Pooh ('silly old bear') can hear the honey pots of his inspiration humming in the distance and find his way home.

## *Homecoming*

When I discovered this college I began to find *my* way home. Partly it was the sheer beauty of the place – the grand old family home of Pixton House, with its flowering shrubs, its sixteen steps down to the lily pond, its wide view over the valley of the River Medway (which borders the college grounds) and the fine, mature oak trees standing in the parkland. Closer up, the smell of home-made bread, the curious crafting of the lampshades, the portrait of Ralph Waldo Emerson in the stairwell, all contributed to my sense of having arrived somewhere.

Underlying these joys, however, was the deep valuing of the imagination that I found among my teachers, without which (I am certain) it is not possible for anyone to feel at home in this world. Elizabeth Edmunds, in particular, was a gracious presence with the gift of being able to see beyond the baggage we brought with us and speak to the secret potential in each person. I have always been grateful for this, and have tried to learn from it in my own meetings with people.

My colleague, John Davy, who taught at this college for many years, once (in his role as Science correspondent for *The Observer*) interviewed the behaviourist philosopher and educator B.F. Skinner about his work. At the end of the conversation Skinner said: 'Well, Mr. Davy, don't think that we have been talking to

Pixton House

each another. We have been merely flapping our lips.' And, indeed, what else could he say? If you hold the view that we consist entirely of behaviour shaped by outer circumstances, then to stake a claim for freedom and human dignity is entirely meaningless. There is nobody at home to claim it. Yes, but throughout this book I do claim it – that whenever imagination comes alive between us, the inwardness and beauty of another person, or of the natural world, will speak its meanings freely.

## Romanticism comes of age

This is my opportunity to make further mention of another of our presiding spirits – Ralph Waldo Emerson, the great philosopher/

poet from New England, after whom this college is named. All his life he was a courageous defender of the life of imagination, of what was obvious to him – that this world has an inside to it:

> For the world is not painted or adorned, but is from the beginning beautiful; and God has not made some beautiful things, but beauty is the creator of the universe.[13]

Such a statement places him in the stream of the Romantic writers who came just a little before him, and who will feature strongly throughout this book (his essay on *Nature*[14] would make a fine accompanying text for what I am presenting here). It is important to note in this context that another philosopher/poet, Owen Barfield, who lived in Forest Row during his last years (and was a good friend of the college), held the view that while the Romantics recognised 'the truth of the imagination', they failed to ask in what way it was true, and as a result their creative vigour declined and the sentimental, painted adornment that Ralph Waldo was wary of took over. It is in Rudolf Steiner's 'anthroposophy', according to Barfield, that Romanticism takes the necessary step and 'comes of age'.[15] Much inspired by the poet/scientist J.W. von Goethe, Steiner shows how imagination can be trained as a conscious faculty.

## What Emerson College stands for

The cultivation of such a life in thinking and perceiving is fundamental to what the college offers. Rudolf Steiner speaks in his *Philosophy of Freedom* of transforming our thinking (so often experienced as cold and detached) into a 'warm, luminous' faculty which 'penetrates deeply into the phenomena of the world'[16] – in other words, it is possible for love to participate in the act of knowing. These things we exercise through study, through observational science and through work with the arts and crafts (whether in general or more specialised courses). With the imagination thus developed we can begin to apprehend the subtleties and the qualities that are speaking to us all the time through the colours, numbers, tones and gestures that surround us. Owen Barfield's word for this, 'participation', will sound repeatedly throughout this book.

Easy to say all this and yet – with our whole culture based on a sense, a belief, an illusion that none of these things have any interior to penetrate into – what we are actually engaged in is a battle for the soul. So much for '*in* the beginning was the Word'. Now, *at* the beginning, a 'Big Bang' is all that we can admit to; and the pain of contemplating such a hollowed out world makes clear to me once again what this college stands for. Do we spend our days banging up against soulless objects and commodities? A little exercise of the faculty that I have been describing would remedy that. It would tell us that all the many outwardnesses listed on the cornflakes packet are not what food is really made of; that history has an inside to it (our unfolding creative story); that the scent and form and colour of a rose do; that the way we move speaks about us; that the language moving between us is more than information technology; that the people we meet are essential characters in the drama of who we are.

I will say it boldly: every aspect of the outer world has an in-side that we can grasp through enlivened thinking. This is a serious matter, with highly practical consequences, and it provides the essential basis for the professional trainings that we offer.[17] If you need convincing about the urgency of this, try imagining what happens when a farmer regards the earth as mere dirt to be dug for profit. And what about the teacher so intent upon filling up empty brains, or climbing rungs on school league tables that he quite forgets to notice the unique individuals who stand before him?

## Spells

My own particular work at the college has been with Creative Writing, adapting my offerings to the needs of teachers, storytellers, students of English, but also developing courses specifically designed to free and then to craft a sense for living language.

In my earlier book, *Sing Me the Creation*,[18] I explored the relationship between language and the human soul (called *Healing the Word* when offered as a writing course). Work deeply enough with the human ideals revealed in grammar and you find yourself engaged in the practice of 'Right Speech' that the Buddha included in his *Eightfold Path*.[19]

The inside-out of that work (and my main purpose in the present book) is to encourage, through Creative Writing, an understanding of and reverence for 'the language of nature' – of minerals, plants, animals – so as to heal our exploitative relationship with those companions and, drawing on the living images and gestures they provide, to find a voice for what lives most deeply inside us.

A permission of language is always a permission of consciousness. From time to time, therefore, you will find me referring to the many writing exercises presented in this book as 'spells', powers in words to carry you across (if you are willing) into that place of imagination from which all true language comes. The related German word 'spiel' means 'play', and it is in this spirit that I seek to engage you, step by step, through writing, drawing and moving, in a transformation of perception and a re-enchantment of the world. The sign X that I use throughout (abbreviation for 'exercise' though it is) may be taken to mark the spot where soul and sense worlds cross, a power of *multiplication* beyond that modern academic tendency which seeks merely to *add* to our store of knowledge. Poetic consciousness, with its care for the relationship between inner and outer experience, is naturally ecological, and to cultivate it is a first step towards healing our present crisis. As the American poet, William Carlos Williams, said 'a new world is only a new mind'.[20]

## *Notes*

[1]   Willard, B., *The Forest*, Sweethaws Press, p.156

[2]   Cobbett, W., *Rural Rides*, Penguin Books, 2001

[3]   Milne, A.A., *The House at Pooh Corner*, Methuen Children's Books, 1973, p.170

[4]   Penn, R., *Portrait of Ashdown Forest*, Robert Hale Ltd. 1984, p.10: map

[5]   Mason Neale, J., 'Good King Wenceslas' in *The Oxford Book of Carols*, Oxford University Press, 1965, p.302

[6]   Jonson, B., *The Poems of Ben Jonson*, Routledge and Kegan Paul, 1962, p.76

[7]   Woolf, V., *A Room of One's Own*, Penguin Books, 2002

[8]   Pound, E., 'Canto LXXXIII' in *The Cantos*, Faber and Faber, 1960, p.569

[9]   Pound, E., in Jones, P., (ed.) *Imagist Poetry*, Penguin Books, 1972, p.141

[10]   Yeats, W.B., *A Vision*, Collier Books, 1966, p.3

[11]   Ibid., p.9

[12]   Milne, A.A., *The House at Pooh Corner*, Methuen Children's Books, 1973, p.128

[13]   Emerson, R.W., Essay on 'The Poet' in *Selected Prose and Poetry*, Holt, Rinehardt and Winston, 1962, p.318

[14]   Emerson, R.W., *Selected Prose and Poetry*, Holt, Rinehardt and Winston, 1962, p.3

[15]   Barfield, O., *Romanticism Comes of Age*, Rudolf Steiner Press, 1966, p.28

[16]   Steiner, R., *The Philosophy of Freedom*, Rudolf Steiner Press, 1964, p.119

[17]   Details of training courses are available from Emerson College, Forest Row, E. Sussex, RH18 5JX

[18]   Matthews, P., *Sing Me the Creation*, Hawthorn Press, 1994

[19]   Bittleston, A., *Our Spiritual Companions*, Floris Books, 1980, p.28

[20]   Williams, W.C., *Pictures from Breughel*, New Directions, 1962, p.76

# Opening our Senses to Each Other and the World

*As we begin our work we open our senses to each other and our environment. This involves some initial word play and collaborative writing, bringing language alive between us and seeking to overcome the inbred expectation that what we write is to be judged and criticised. Brief excursions outside with a companion, and writing from direct observation of whatever we encounter, lead into a consideration of what imagination is, and the suggestion that it is closely linked to the development of our sense perception. We explore ways in writing to discover afresh the purity and clarity of seeing which we possessed in childhood. We end with the question of how close up to nature we can get through language.*

Upon welcoming, in the presence of the whole community, those who had come to work with me, I spoke a few spring poems – innocent ones from a few hundred years ago, filled with birdsong. Here is the first verse of one by Thomas Nashe:

> Spring, the sweet spring, is the year's pleasant king,
> Then blooms each thing, then maids dance in a ring,
> Cold doth not sting, the pretty birds do sing:
> Cuckoo, jug-jug, pu-we, to-witta-woo![1]

And then, in contrast, a more modern one, 'Spring', by Edna St.

Vincent Millay, mistrustful of the over-exuberance of life forces at this time of year:

> To what purpose, April, do you return again?
> Beauty is not enough.
> You can no longer quiet me with the redness
> Of little leaves opening stickily.
> I know what I know.
> The sun is hot on my neck as I observe
> The spikes of the crocus.
> The smell of the earth is good.
> It is apparent that there is no death.
> But what does that signify?
> Not only under ground are the brains of men
> Eaten by maggots,
> Life in itself
> Is nothing,
> An empty cup, a flight of uncarpeted stairs.
> It is not enough that yearly, down this hill,
> April
> Comes like an idiot, babbling and strewing flowers.[2]

Her reference to the maggots that wind their way through the brains of the living, ugly though it is, implies the possibility of overcoming death through finding superabundant life within our thinking.

## *Beginning our work together*

Later in the morning when the group first gathered in the 'Speech and Drama Hut' (our home space) we shared our names and aims: some certainly had ambitions to be writers, but needed to find a way of unblocking stuck places. Some said they had been so long involved with informational writing that they needed to balance this with the creative. One wanted to see how I worked socially with language in the group in order to take skills back into her social and therapeutic work. Others were preparing to be teachers or to work with children, a realm where the use of living language is so essential. Some were simply searching, or wanting to enjoy themselves (I'm sure I never mentioned that in the course brochure).

The walls of our hut were bare and open. I had deliberately left them so, except for a reproduction of Botticelli's *Primavera*,[3] which I had hung beside our working area.

I thought I knew this work, but when somebody pointed out that 'Prima Vera' means not just 'spring' but 'first truth' we began, in a first spontaneous act of observation and imagination, to discover all manner of secrets in the painting: how the energy in it moves from right to left – from the wild energy of March, through the wild flowering (Flora) of April, into May (represented by Venus); how at that point Venus looks out of the picture towards the viewer, seeking to engage us in the emerging process; how thereby the given energy is harmonised, passing through the dance of the Three Graces into June, where Mercury (with his Caduceus, pruning knife, and winged sandals) brings order into the vegetation and the weather. Between the blue of March and the red of Mercury stands Venus who gathers the red and the blue together in her heart. Find a more colourful copy of it if you can, for, while not dismissing Millay's perception of April as an *idiot*, it invites us to participate in the dance of springtime with our thoughtful and co-creative attention.

At this point we picked up our pens for the first time, and as a seed for these nine weeks together I asked each person to catch the momentum of this first moment and...

## X 1.   Write one word

I then called upon everyone to speak their word, and to speak it again each time I beckoned towards them. In this way the words were gradually introduced to the group and to each other. 'Travel' and 'Happy' were the first words that came – 'to travel happy', that seemed a good omen for our journey. 'Happy Warmth', 'Open Warmth', 'Life Open', 'Open Happy Life', 'Open Travel', 'Life Travel' – these were some of the words we received this first morning. Not many concrete nouns. All rather hopeful and Romantic. 'Fresh Apricot Song.'

# *Haiku*

This attention for the word in its fit place and time is essential to the writing of haiku. I sometimes feel hesitant about introducing this form in English, for so clearly it grows out of a particular language and culture, out of a consciousness that we can only approximate to in the West. I have, however, had many Japanese students over the years, and have done my best to learn from them. One of them even taught me to speak the original of Basho's famous poem about the frog jumping into the pond:

> Furuike-ya
> kawazu tobikomu
> mizu no oto.[4]

What is more, it is almost one hundred years since Ezra Pound began experimenting with the form in English up there in Stone Cottage; so hopefully I have ground enough underfoot to attempt it. It is not for nothing that the haiku form has become popular in the west. In our time of rushing from one impression to the next we have much to learn from such an exquisite hearkening to the nuances and innuendoes of the passing moment.

We were able to gather from the group the main features of this poetic form: a 17-syllable poem, three lines long – 5 syllables, 7 syllables, 5 syllables. Each haiku must have a hint of the season, catching an essence of both place and moment. We shared our favourite examples:

> Little grasshopper –
> shelter from the midnight frost
> in the scarecrow's sleeve.[5]

*Christopher Logue*
*(This one has the right syllable count)*

\*

> Don't cry, little insects!
> Even the loving stars
> will someday separate.[6]

*Issa*
*(Note the tension between cosmic and particular)*

\*

> The temple bells have stopped
> but the sound keeps coming
> out of the flowers.[7]

*Basho*
*(Everything that lives is holy)*

This is the handbell hung in the courtyard behind Pixton House. It has 'Ring for attention' written beside it. Once when I rang it a family of moths flew out to attend to me.

'The trouble with most poetry', said Basho, 'is that it is either subjective or objective.' But in the following example, particularly, these two extremes come together or are transcended through a simple description of an outer event which actually embodies idea and feeling without ever making it explicit:

> Wild Persimmons –
> the mother eating
> the bitter parts.[8]

*Issa*
*(The scene becomes its symbol)*

## X 2.    Write some haiku, in alternate lines with a partner

Today it's snowing.
At the fireplace I knit
for friends no longer here.

Here (with translation help from Japanese friends) is a description by one of Basho's disciples of how the famous frog poem was created:

The Master of Basho-an had been lamenting all day that poets were always expressing 'fuga' (the beauty of the poem) as if it were a piece of cloud blown by the wind, taking now the form of a dog, then of a white cloth – but without any truth between them.

He stopped his contemplation and came back to himself – it was the spring nearly ending there. It was raining quietly, so the cooing of a pigeon sounded deeply. In the gentle wind, petals of cherry blossom were drifting slowly down. It was the time in late March when we regret that spring is passing and we cherish the memory of it. Now and then the sound of frogs jumping into water was heard. Then an air of something beyond words came over him, and he realised the second half of the poem:

'A frog is jumping into
the sound of water'

Fushi who was with him suggested for the first half:

'The yellow rose'

But he decided upon:

'An old pond'

> Certainly 'the yellow rose' is refined and beautiful, but 'an old pond', being simpler, holds more 'jitsu' (the truth which runs through all the ages). Only the deepest of hearts could achieve it.[9]

The comparison of the suggested line with Basho's final choice illustrates very well the difference between description and evocation. It is a fine example of a true image as defined by Ezra Pound, in that it presents 'an intellectual and emotional complex in an instant of time'.[10] It also points towards the Japanese practice of collaborative composition (which has inspired me in my work with groups), and to Renga, which is the collaborative writing of linked haiku. My collaborators in translation leave an ambiguity as to whether the frog is jumping into water or into the sound that water makes when frogs jump into it, and I am reluctant to edit out this delightful, if unintended, co-existence of meanings.

### Basho's Old Green Pond

A lot of us know you let a frog jump in. You told the story well. Famously, even. But he's been jumping in, to the benefit of your haiku, for 400 years, give or take. Don't you think you could let the poor creature do something else? He'd be so eager, by now, to jump back out. I bet he could do it in less than 17 syllables. Let him try, Basho. The time is right.[11]

*Owen Davis*

When Basho was dying and too ill to speak he was seen to be counting syllables on his fingers, though I can hardly believe he needed to when the form was so much in him. Perhaps he was leaving us with the ultimate silent haiku.

# *A haiku hike*

X 3.  Take a walk with a companion. Carry pen and paper with you, sharing eyes and ears for the things and events and meetings that come to you along the way. Point them out to each other. Write them down. If you then share them occasionally with your companion it might inspire some written response. There's no need to write haiku, but carry the mood of it – of listening, even with your eyes.

Upon return from that walk move around the room, sharing some of these small pieces with the people you happen to bump into.

X 4.  If any of the pieces are tending towards haiku, try to perfect them overnight:

> Oh, how can I drive
> with all this cherry blossom
> covering the windshield?
>
> *PM*

It was Basho's practice to write haiku as he travelled with a companion on 'the narrow road to the deep North'.[12] Upon his return he wrote an account of the journey, placing each of those fleeting impressions into their context – moment and memory coming together.

X 5.  Write an individual piece, a travelogue based on the walk you shared together, and include in it some of the haiku-type pieces that you wrote:

> M and I went for a walk. We had only taken a few steps when we stopped under the cherry tree. A man with a blue bag

raised his eyebrow as he walked past us. I was eager to keep moving, but M stood rooted to the place. That's when a drop of rain fell from a twig onto her neck and splashed her notebook. She looked up then, and soon we were walking up the path. I remembered something L said about being so busy trying to get into the 'secret garden' that we fail to notice that we are there already. M confessed that the task of carrying pens out into nature made her feel inferior, and I (being an over-anxious teacher) said, well, we must accept that as part of the adventure:

Yes, yes, but the Thrush
does it so much better
with his unscripted song.

*PM*

Probably this too is best done with a night's sleep between to allow the immediate events to be somewhat 'recollected in tranquillity' (see p.54). We shared our travelogues, first with our walking partner, comparing our experiences, and then in the whole group.

## X 6.  The same task can be done in written collaboration with your walking partner:

What was the first thing we met when we stepped outside?

I could feel fresh air. Birds were singing. It made me laugh.

Yes, and beside the path we found a silver birch tree. But you told me its real name.

'Dan Pang Namu', is what I said.

And do you remember the big brown leaf we found?
Of course I do. We gave it to Eran and he was smiling.

You were laughing. Eran was smiling. And then a boy blew a kiss to you through the branches of the apple tree.

Yes, he blew a kiss to me, even though I didn't know him at all. Then we found some flowers called 'Forget-Me-Not'. I said, 'I will miss you.'

Soon we came to a red hut where two women were pretending not to be poets.

We found a sign on the door.

We knocked twice, but the people inside were pretending not to be at home. Then I asked you to discover something no one had ever seen in the world before.

I said – I don't know what. Then:

This spider web
in the doorway. Nobody
had eyes for it, 'til now.

You told me that wife-spider eats her husband. I couldn't believe it. Oh my God!

Yes, my dear – spring time is not just for laughing.

*PM with Yun Hee Kim*

'Pretending not to be poets'? Basho has this to say about the wandering poet:

> I wandered out onto the road at last one day this past autumn, possessed by an irresistible desire to see the rise of the full moon over the mountains of the Kashima Shrine. I was accompanied by two men. One was a masterless youth, and the other was a wandering priest. The latter was clad in a robe black as a crow, with a bundle of sacred stoles around his neck and on his back a portable shrine containing a holy image of the Buddha-after-enlightenment. This priest, brandishing his long staff, stepped into the road, ahead of all the others, as if he had a free pass to the World beyond the Gateless Gate. I, too, was clad in a black robe, but neither a priest nor an ordinary man of this world was I, for I wavered ceaselessly, like a bat, that passes for a bird at one time and for a mouse at another.[13]

## What is imagination?

Having opened up this theme of *working with imagination* it seemed important to ask:

X 7.   **What is imagination? Write one sentence in answer to this basic question. Then you can gather them:**

- Imagination is seeing pictures that the world's heart has wished for.
- Imagination is the ability to be part of the Creation as a creator.
- It is a breathing-in to things, entering into an inner dialogue with the world.
- Imagination is mischievous, lying dormant and emerging without warning.

- Imagination is throwing your heart over the stream and trusting your body to follow.
- To be imaginative is to be present in the presence of things.
- Imagination shows us the inside of the world and the outside of the mind.
- Imagination is the nation shared by all.
- A life without imagination? I can't imagine it.

*Loise Coe, Angie Montagu, Luci Sale*

It is a list that we will be adding to throughout our work together.

When we shared what we had written, a question arose concerning the relationship between expression and communication. Owen Barfield has this to say about it:

> Language has two primary functions, one of which is expression and the other is communication. They are not the only functions language performs, but they are both indispensable to its existence. The goal to which expression aspires… is something like fullness or sincerity. The goal to which communication aspires is accuracy. Both functions must be performed in some degree – and at the same time – otherwise there is no language at all. But the extent to which either function predominates over the other will vary greatly.[14]

What Barfield says about fullness and accuracy can be illustrated simply through the following example:

| EXPRESSION | COMMUNICATION |
| --- | --- |
| (Oh! Wow!) | (Two plus two equals four) |

Expressive language, however, can go beyond fullness, into beauty. And accurate communication can be taken further, into the speaking of wisdom and truth.

The question arising in the group came out of the pain of being too long trapped in the purely communicative mode while, at the same time, wondering whether the expressive (creative?) mode can be trusted. I was very grateful to receive that question, for it immediately brought before us a theme central to the whole work of the course - the relationship between beauty and truth, between art and science. It is the question, surely, at the heart of the creative writer's art: How can imagination serve the truth?

**X 8.   A more playful way of exploring 'imagination' is to make an acrostic of it:**

| Imagination | Imagination | Imagination |
|---|---|---|
| Means | Means | Makes |
| A | A | A |
| Generous | Genius | Gentleman |
| Interaction – | Is | Into |
| Nature | Now | Nobody |
| And | Allowed | And |
| Thinker | To | Then |
| Inside | Inhabit | It |
| Out | Our | Opens |
| Now | Names | Newness |

The verbs that spontaneously arise – *open, make, allow, interact, inhabit* – are particularly instructive.

Here is William Blake's spirited defence of the truth of imagination:

> I see everything that I paint in This World, but Everybody does not see alike. To the Eyes of a Miser a Guinea is more beautiful than the Sun, and a bag worn with the use of Money has more beautiful proportions than a Vine filled with Grapes. The tree

which moves some to tears of joy is in the eyes of others only a green thing that stands in the way. Some see Nature all Ridicule and Deformity, and by these I shall not regulate my proportions; and some scarce see Nature at all. But to the Eyes of the Man of Imagination, Nature is Imagination itself. As a Man is, so he sees. As the eye is formed, such are its powers. You certainly mistake, when you say that the Visions of Fancy are not to be found in This World. To me this world is one continued Vision of Fancy or Imagination.[15]

It is clear that for Blake the imaginative life is an enhancement rather than a denial of sense experience, the senses for him being 'the chief inlets of soul for this Age'.[16] He has many other pithy things to say about imagination and the senses; we will weave them in from time to time. Meanwhile, here is a diagram, drawn from Rudolf Steiner's researches, which points to twelve human senses, some of them known to us, some not so easily recognisable:

## *Our twelve senses*

Our sense organs stand as twelve windows between self and world. In the following diagram Rudolf Steiner distinguishes three realms of perception, and three groups of senses that particularly serve them:

| **Our own body:** | **The outer world:** | **The other person:** |
|---|---|---|
| Balance | Warmth | Ego |
| Movement | Sight | Thought |
| Well-being | Smell | Word |
| Touch | Taste | Hearing |

You could also call them senses of body, soul and spirit, respectively; or relate them to our faculties of will, feeling and thinking. Steiner loves such formulations,[17] and yet just when you think you've got it clear, he dissolves it again and shapes it some other way. Twelve? Try adding some of your own if you like.

The diagonal lines indicate cross-connections, the body senses on the left being regarded as the basis for the less tangible senses in the right hand column. The meeting of ego to ego confirmed in a handshake – that feels real to me, as does the relationship of word to movement which you will find repeatedly entering these pages. Balance and hearing? The semi-circular canals, which act as a spirit level to keep us upright, are located in the ear. None of the senses, in fact, work in isolation. One cold night I was astonished to find that when I took my hat away from my ears the stars twinkled more brightly. 'The senses do not deceive, but the judgement deceives',[18] said Goethe, and: 'The human being is adequately equipped for all true earthly requirements if he trusts his senses, and so develops them as to make them worthy of trust.'[19] Parents and teachers, if we are lucky, help us develop our senses in childhood. Later, working with the arts – music, painting, dancing, cooking, sculpture, poetry – we can bring our own awareness to bear on nurturing and ensouling them.

X 9.   Chose a partner and go for another walk, this time with someone who, blindfolded, is willing to be led by a simple holding of hands. The one guiding will need to carry eyes for the two of you, allowing the other to attend to the journey through more subtle senses. Walk basically in silence, and even when you arrive home don't speak much about this shared event, but savour it as content for the next step in the process.

X 10.  Transcribe your walk, including its time-sequence and observational details, but also revealing feelings and inward responses to that shared experience (it could, alternatively, be done in written conversation with your walking partner):

On Wednesday we went outside in pairs. I went with Ines. I was blindfolded and she was my guide. First she turned me around gently a few times. But I could figure out what direction we were going anyway. I thought I would be trying to know where I was all the time, but after just a few seconds it didn't matter. I could hear the wind because of the trees, and soon it seemed that the sound was a roof over my head that was high sometimes and lower sometimes. My boots had thick soles, but I could tell if I was walking on the ground, or gravel or cement, or the lawn by the sound and by the resistance under my feet. Ines led me gently around for a while, then stopped and brought my hand to touch something. The first thing was close to the ground and had leaves that contained some moisture because they resisted my touch a bit. They felt like skin and I realised that the sensation was somewhat erotic. Then she led me to something else. It was the trunk of a tree. It made me gasp to feel it; each time something new was brought to my hand, I found that I gasped. This trunk was rather smooth, although there was much small roughness all over it. I found that I could put my arms entirely around it. Then I moved my hands up further, and found the branches that forked from the trunk. It was like touching someone's body – someone who had his or her hands raised up in the air. The air was moving almost constantly and was the sound I was most aware of, although I noticed birds, and other people's footsteps, and other sounds from time to time. The air was no longer the empty space between me and something solid, but was a very present physical thing in itself. It, like the other things that I heard or touched or smelled, came to me and gave me gifts of sensations. When I was walking, sensations came to my ears, but also very much to my skin, my hair, my face. It was something like physical love, but finer (more subtle) and larger. After a while it was no longer erotic, but very moving. I felt on the edge of tears all the time.

At one point Ines had me touch someone else's hands. They were small with tapered fingers. I thought by that that it might be Vivienne. I felt the face, which was blindfolded, and the chin, which was narrow and tapered as well, and knew that it was Vivienne. I said her name, and she said mine. Nearly every sensation was in my whole body, and not just my ears or fingers or nose. When I was being led, I didn't want to hold myself narrow, but wide, so I could be ready. It seemed that I was breathing with my whole body... I was led back to Ines. After not very long she led me to a place and let go of my hand. She slowly undid the blindfold and pulled it away from my eyes. The impact of sight and colour was so strong I can't say it. I saw blue-purple and copper-red and green mostly. It was like a powerful blow to my heart, and I began crying. Ines said, 'I'm sorry'. Later she said she thought she had hurt me, but that wasn't it at all. And I felt that she had sacrificed something so that I could have this experience. I was very grateful... It was one of the most powerful experiences I have ever had. I don't know how to say it right.

*Christine Meyer*

We still had time at the end of the morning to share with the others in the group what we had written. I was listening for the balance between outer observation and expression of inwardness, for it seems to me that imagination is much more grounded in observation than we usually realise. Often when people come to

Creative Writing they try so hard to be imaginative that they end up being only imaginary, inventing worlds rather than trusting that this world is indeed 'one continued Vision of Fancy or Imagination' (see p.39). No need to force it. The honest naming of what is immediately in front of us can make things shine in an extraordinary light.

The French poet, Arthur Rimbaud, feeling (as a young man) trapped by the limitations of the senses said, 'The poet makes himself a Seer by a long, prodigious and rational disordering of the senses',[20] and began experimenting with synaesthesic images in which one realm of sense perception is expressed in terms of another:

> And from that time on I bathed in the Poem of the sea, star-infused and churned into milk, devouring the green azure... I have struck, do you realise, incredible Floridas, where mingle with flowers the eyes of panthers in human skins.[21]

He longs to include the 'outer world' of rocks and plants and creatures within the boundaries of his 'human skin', and a 'disordering' of the senses seems the only available way. The 'ensouling' of them, that I am proposing here, is another means, and probably safer.

> If the doors of perception were cleansed we would see everything as it is – Infinite.[22]
>
> *William Blake*

> The eye is formed by light and for the light so that the inner light may emerge to meet the outer light.[23]
>
> *J.W. von Goethe*

X 11.   I am sure you can devise writing tasks of your own which arise through giving your attention to the world through other senses. Smell, taste, touch, hearing provide obvious ways in. Experiments in synaesthesia (described above) could be part of it.

## *The Imagist movement*

I have noted already that in the winters of 1912, 1913 and 1914 Ezra Pound was doing an important literary work in Stone Cottage, and sometimes drinking cider with W.B. Yeats in the Hatch Inn down the road.

Here is Yeats's 'Drinking Song':

> Wine comes in at the mouth
> And love comes in at the eye.
> That's all we shall know for truth
> Before we grow old and die.
> I lift the glass to my mouth.
> I look at you, and I sigh.[24]

The Hatch Inn

He surely did not write it there, but whenever I drink there with friends I like to recite it. I don't suppose Pound would have liked it. He wrote several letters from Coleman's Hatch encouraging the writing of 'free verse', and promoting the *Imagist* movement that he named and founded. Central to its doctrine was 'Phanopoeia' – the ability to cast images upon the mind; and what better school to turn to for its development than the Japanese and Chinese poetry which was beginning to find its way to the West. Pound had been presented with an essay by the late Ernest Fenollosa which so impressed him that he published it as *The Chinese Written Character as a Medium for Poetry*.[25] Those knowledgeable in the field were quick to criticise it as being incorrect and unscholarly, but it remains nonetheless a vital text for poetic practice, advocating what is now basic to modern Creative Writing courses – that, rather than 'telling' of your emotion, it is more effective to evoke and interpret it for the reader. This sound advice for writers (a cure, in Pound's view, for the 'emotional slither' so rampant in English poetry) moves in Pound at his best into a sacramental view of the world in which idea and spirit are apprehended within created things. As one contemporary commentator, May Sinclair, saw it: 'The Imagists… believe in Transubstantiation… for them the bread and the wine are the body and blood'[26]– not just symbols of reality.

During his time at Stone Cottage Ezra Pound was preparing one of his most enduring books, *Cathay*,[27] a collection of poems freely worked from Fenollosa's notes and translations into fine English poems. The greatest of them, perhaps, is this:

### The River Merchant's Wife: A Letter

While my hair was still cut straight across my forehead
I played about the front gate, pulling flowers.
You came by on bamboo stilts, playing horse,
You walked by my seat, playing with blue plums.
And we went on living in the village of Chokan:
Two small people, without dislike or suspicion.

At fourteen I married my Lord you.
I never laughed, being bashful.
Lowering my head, I looked at the wall.
Called to a thousand times, I never looked back.

At fifteen I stopped scowling,
I desired my dust to be mingled with yours
For ever and for ever and for ever.
Why should I climb the lookout?

At sixteen you departed,
You went into far Ku-to-yen, by the river of swirling eddies.
And you have been gone five months.
The monkeys make sorrowful noise overhead.

You dragged your feet when you went out.
By the gate now, the moss is grown, the different mosses,
Too deep to clear them away!
The leaves fall early this autumn, in wind.

The paired butterflies are already yellow with August
Over the grass in the West garden.
They hurt me. I grow older.
If you are coming down through the narrows of the river Kiang,
Please let me know beforehand,
And I will come out to meet you
        As far as Cho-fu-sa.[28]

Notice how the things and happenings of the world interpret the inner drama – not 'How sad I am' but, 'The monkeys make sorrowful noise overhead.' Some people think that those beautiful lines about the butterflies are more aptly applied to the garden at Stone Cottage than to far-off China where Li Po wrote the original.[29]

# *The language of childhood*

Today we took as the focus of our conversation Christ's saying that 'unless ye become as little children ye shall not enter into the kingdom of heaven.'[30] Meek obedience to the will of God – is that what it means? The 17th century mystic, Thomas Traherne, has a different take on it, saying that if we could find once again the freshness of perception that we had in childhood then the 'kingdom' would be here, now, between us, all around:

> The corn was orient and immortal wheat, which never should be reaped, nor was ever sown. I thought it had stood from everlasting to everlasting. The dust and stones of the street were as precious as gold: the gates were at first the end of the world. The green trees when I saw them first through one of the gates transported and ravished me, their sweetness and unusual beauty made my heart to leap, and almost mad with ecstasy, they were such strange and wonderful things. The Men! O what venerable and reverend creatures did the aged seem! Immortal Cherubims! And young men glittering and sparkling Angels, and maids strange seraphic pieces of life and beauty! Boys and girls tumbling, and playing, were moving jewels. I knew not that they were born or should die; but all things abided eternally as they were in their proper places. Eternity was manifest in the Light of Day, and something infinite behind everything appeared: which talked with my expectation and moved my desire. The city seemed to stand in Eden, or to be built in Heaven. The streets were mine, the temple was mine, the people were mine, their clothes and gold and silver were mine, as much as their sparkling eyes, fair skins and ruddy faces. The skies were mine, and so were the sun and moon and stars, and all the World was mine; and I the only spectator and enjoyer of it. I knew no churlish proprieties, nor

bounds, nor divisions: but all proprieties and divisions were mine: all treasures and the possessors of them. So that with much ado I was corrupted, and made to learn the dirty devices of this world. Which now I unlearn, and become, as it were, a little child again that I may enter into the Kingdom of God.[31]

And here are two poems by children that arise out of such unlearnedness:[32]

I feel a bit happier
when I see a Kingfisher
in the spring green willows
and the oak-leaved ferns
by the Lemonwood trees.

*Clifton Roderick Foster, age 11*

This first one is an immediate feeling response (without *emotional slither*) to the perceived world. The second one, free of any conscious literary intent, is another fine example of how a simple observed detail can interpret a rich depth of feeling and meaning:

See this beautiful rainy day
that waters the pretty flowers
and washes away my hopscotch.

*Alliene Grover, age 7*

It strikes me how similar this is to the images in Li Po's poem about the loss of childhood (see p.46).

It would be artificial for us to merely imitate such songs of innocence. Here, however, is a language task that (while not denying our state of *experience*) shows a way in to that spirit of imagination that belongs so delightfully to the kingdom of childhood:

**X 12.  Go outside to a place of activity, and record outer impressions and inner responses in words of one syllable:**

I came to the edge of a wood.
Down through Birch boughs
I could see lake shine.
Up where I stood
the not-yet-leaves were in the twig.
Sun on the white bark coaxed them out.
Wren song cussed and called them.

Wind will shake each leaf type
its own true way.
Let it shake me my way.
No hand can catch the Thrush
that sings and sings as though now
were the only time.

*PM*

(For a more energetic example, see p.76)

Reflecting on the experience afterwards, we agreed that what seems at first to be a limitation of language can actually be a means of freeing us from 'the lethargy of custom' (see p.90) that clings to our adult perception. Noticeably, the task invites us to use pictorial and will-full words drawn from the Saxon, rather than the more thoughtful and detached Latin roots of our language.

## Songs of innocence

So often when we take our pens out into nature the world seems unwilling to accept our language. This separateness can be very painful. It does, however, belong to our modern, adult, western experience. We cannot merely shake it off but, acknowledging the pain of it, look for a way through. William Blake in his introductory poem to the *Songs of Innocence* (which you will notice has no words of more than two syllables) points to an earlier, more participating consciousness:

> Piping down the valleys wild,
> Piping songs of pleasant glee,
> On a cloud I saw a child,
> And he laughing said to me:
>
> 'Pipe a song about a Lamb!'
> So I piped with merry chear.
> 'Piper, pipe that song again.'
> So I piped: he wept to hear.
>
> 'Drop thy pipe, thy happy pipe;
> Sing thy songs of happy chear.'
> So I sung the same again,
> While he wept with joy to hear.

'Piper, sit thee down and write
In a book that all may read.'
So he vanish'd from my sight,
And I plucked a hollow reed,

And I made a rural pen,
And I stained the water clear,
And I wrote my happy songs
Every child may joy to hear.[33]

True, the poem indicates a shift from the oral poetry of childhood and pre-literate times towards the written. Even so, the pen is not imported into nature, but found there. The act of writing does, however, entail a vanishing of the source of inspiration and a slight darkening of the water (a touch, perhaps, of Blake's more sombre vision of the realm of *experience*). At the end, though, what has been written is lifted off the page in song and accepted once more into the living air.

## *Wild eye*

This theme of childhood was dear to other English Romantic poets of the late 18th and early 19th centuries, inspired as they were by the doctrines of Jean-Jacques Rousseau who, upholding the notion of the 'Noble Savage',[34] advocated that children should be brought up among the moral influences of nature. It turned out to be something of a sentimental doctrine which did not take into account the darker recesses of human nature, yet a famous example of someone who benefited from such an upbringing and retained a childlike eye into adulthood is Dorothy Wordsworth, the sister of the poet William. Here, in one of her journal entries, she embodies the 'real language of men'[35] that the Romantics (in turning away from the artificial language of court and university) were looking for:

(April 15)

It was a threatening misty morning, but mild… When we were in the woods close to Gowbarrow Park we saw a few daffodils close to the water-side. We fancied that the sea had floated the seeds ashore, and that the little colony had so sprung up. But as we went along there were more, and yet more; and, at last, under the boughs of the trees, we saw that there was a long belt of them along the shore, about the breadth of a country turnpike road. I never saw daffodils so beautiful. They grew among the mossy stones about and above them; some rested their heads upon these stones, as on a pillow, for weariness; and the rest tossed and reeled and danced, and seemed as if they verily laughed with the wind, that blew upon them over the lake; they looked so gay, ever glancing, ever changing. This wind blew directly over the lake to them. There was here and there a little knot, and a few stragglers higher up; but they were so few as not to disturb the simplicity, unity of life of that one busy highway.[36]

Notice how Dorothy, too, uses so many words of just one syllable.

Coming towards the end of our first week's work together, we looked at this passage in the group, and then (as many students of English literature have done before) compared it to her brother William's poem 'Daffodils' (see below). The day that we were studying these things just happened to be April 15th (the date of Dorothy's original journal entry), so we thought that before we cast a cold eye over the text we should actually look at a daffodil ourselves. Luckily there were some under the willow tree, just outside. First we named them in the languages that we knew – *Jonquil. Narcissus. Daffodil.* Then we tried to observe whether the same 'glee' arose for us in their presence as it did for William Wordsworth so many springs ago. I am not sure what the opposite of 'glee' is, but one member of the group (drilled with that poem from an early age) certainly suffered it. And so the question arises – does feeling tell truly about the quality of the world, or only about ourselves?

### Daffodils

I wandered lonely as a cloud
That floats on high o'er vales and hills,
When all at once I saw a crowd,
A host of golden daffodils;
Beside the lake, beneath the trees,
Fluttering and dancing in the breeze.

Continuous as the stars that shine
And twinkle on the milky way,
They stretched in never-ending line
Along the margin of a bay;
Ten thousand saw I at a glance,
Tossing their heads in sprightly dance.

The waves beside them danced; but they
Out-did the sparkling waves in glee;
A poet could not but be gay,
In such a jocund company;
I gazed – and gazed – but little thought
What wealth the show to me had brought;

For oft, when on my couch I lie
In vacant or in pensive mood,
They flash upon that inward eye
Which is the bliss of solitude;
And then my heart with pleasure fills
And dances with the daffodils.[37]

*William Wordsworth*

We have seen already (p.32) that to study differences is useful in the learning process, and the comparison here of journal entry and poem brings out the difference between Dorothy's immediate, childlike perception and William's more reflective inward eye. In his *Preface to the Lyrical Ballads* he says this:

> I have said that poetry is the spontaneous overflow of powerful feelings; it takes its origin from emotion recollected in tranquillity: the emotion is contemplated till, by a species of reaction, the tranquillity gradually disappears, and an emotion, kindred to that which was before the subject of contemplation, is gradually produced, and does itself actually exist in the mind. In this mood successful composition generally begins.[38]

His greatest poetry arose out of that source. He could not have achieved it, however, had destiny not blessed him with such a wild-eyed sister.

## On being vulnerable

The Romantic poets (as did Basho) were always taking walking tours with their friends. In reviewing our week's work we recalled the walks we, too, had taken and the writings that arose from it. Some of us, it emerged, had been finding that our collaborative writing brought up feelings of being inadequate. There is no denying that working with language in a group can be a somewhat naked affair, for the artistic medium that we are working with is the very medium of our social interaction, and any difficulties in that realm will immediately show in the writing that arises between us. People find themselves wishing they could write as beautifully and imaginatively as somebody else. This is an entirely understandable emotion, and one that could even prove useful if we take the next step and ask that person to write with us so that we too can acquire some of that longed-for word magic. In the end, though, we all have our own unique voice to hone and stay true to. Once such vulnerabilities are acknowledged in the group, the resulting care for each other's aims and inadequacies allows a depth of language to be tapped that was not available before.

## *It, you and I*

Here is one further writing task to help open our senses to the world:[39]

X 13.   Go out into the world in groups of three and, when you have found one human-made object (not a work of art), spend some time in its presence, observing it through your various senses and taking note of its particular physical and human environment. Having done this, let one member of the group write about *It*; another address it as *You*; and the third lend it a voice and speak for it as *I*. Or you could try all these modes in turn, starting with the most external.

### A Spoon

It:   Here is a spoon. It is lying outside on a table. It has been out all night. I know this because a drop of rain has gathered in its upturned hollow. Rainwater flecked with milk. A soup spoon. Colour of silver. This spoon only touches the table at two points – at the tip of its handle and at the underside of the deepest point of its bowl. The handle slants diagonally towards the edge of the table. A yellow leaf is lying beside it at the same angle – its stem pointing the same way, its concave face turned upwards. Both spoon and leaf reflect the sun. A spoon filled with morning sunlight after a night of rain.

What a 'boring' task, some will sigh, and certainly the danger is that we define the thing to death; that it dies into noun. Yet this initial sacrifice of standing back from the world, not imposing our emotions or symbolisms upon things but respecting their otherness, is essential if we are ever to know them truly. Often the one who takes this role in the task will describe the object as 'lonely', when actually it is their own experience of separate identity that is being mirrored back to them. This is the pain, but also the gift it gives. It seems, at first, to be a renunciation of any poetic engagement with the world; but the strange thing is that if we do manage to let a spoon be just a spoon, then, when the time is ripe, it will more readily make itself available as unsentimental interpreter of our deepest feelings.

> **You:** It is already warm here in the sunshine, yet how cold you feel against the back of my hand! Some spoons turn my face upside down when I look into them. But you... you are just too dirty to reflect anything! Except the sun! Who left you out all night? What dish ran away with you, and then abandoned you at just this angle? You are not just a spoon, Spoon. You are a whole story – though the two words printed on your side tell only a small part of it. 'Taiwan' is one of them. 'Stainless' is the other. This large milky fingerprint on your inside surface is all that prevents you from betraying the stains on my face this bright morning.

This permission to address the world as 'you' allows our life of feeling (and its lively servant, the adjective) to come flooding in. It is important to keep the task linked to the details of external observation, but to add now a further attention – to our relationship with the object, to the feelings that arise as we stand in its presence. It takes practice to sift what belongs to me (that, too, can be named) from the qualities that belong to the object;

but with perseverance we can train our feelings to be perceptive for the meanings that reside even in humble things.

> **I:**    I am all spoon. Others may prod or slice if they wish. My work is to scoop and serve. To lift food to your mouth. To lift grace to your eye. For, yes, long before you took me by the handle, the wink of my silver caught your attention. Cut no lip, curve yourself round, serve sippers and gulpers alike, are the laws I was born with. Nightlong I mirrored the Milky Way. Then the clouds came. This drop of rain is all I can serve you this morning.

To lend a voice so that seemingly inarticulate things can find utterance is no mere 'literary device' but, potentially, one of the deepest human acts. It implies intuition – the ability to know something from the inside out. Is that impossible? It certainly is, unless love is involved in the act of knowing. But if love is present… then we can begin to stand within the verb of the thing, the creative intention involved in its forging.

In summary: something like this, maybe, though I don't insist on it:

| **Noun** | **Adjective** | **Verb** |
|:---:|:---:|:---:|
| It | You | I |
| Thinking | Feeling | Doing |

It has long been a question for me how close up to the world can we get, and do the things we write about really accept our language? Here, three simple steps of grammar (from *it* to *you* to *I*) show us a path towards such a participation. My own experience is that if you do the task faithfully, without trying too hard to be literary, then the common objects of the household become charged once again with the wonder that we knew in childhood, enhanced within our loving attention and through the words we touch them with.

What we have practised here in relationship to human-made objects will be deepened in our further work with the different realms of nature, and through our study of fairy tale.

## *Notes*

1   Nashe, T., in Abrams, M.H., (ed.) *Norton Anthology of English Literature*, Norton and Co., 1993, p.1006

2   St. Vincent Millay, E., 'Spring' in *Second April*, Michell Kennerley, 1921

3   Botticelli, S., *Primavera*, in the Uffizzi Gallery, Florence, c. 1478

4   Basho, M., 1644-94

5   Logue, C., *Songs*, Hutchinson and Co., 1962

6   Issa, Y., 1762 -1826

7   Basho, M.

8   Issa, Y., trans. by Blythe, R.H.

9   Shiko, 1665- 1731, *Kuzu no Matsubara*

10  Pound, E., in Jones, P., (ed.) *Imagist Poetry*, Penguin Books, 1972

11  Davis, O., in Ramsay, J., (ed.) *Into the Further Reaches*, PS Avalon, 2007, p.57

12  Basho, M., *The Narrow Road to the Deep North*, Penguin Books, 1966

13  Ibid., p.65

14  Barfield, O., *Speakers' Meaning*, Rudolf Steiner Press, 1967, p.35

15  Blake, W., *Complete Writings*, Oxford University Press, 1972, p.793

16  Ibid., p.793

17  Steiner, R., *The Study of Man*, Rudolf Steiner Press, 1981, Ch.8

18  von Goethe, J.W., *Man or Matter*, Ernst Lehrs, Faber and Faber, 1958, p.85

19  Ibid.

20  Rimbaud, A., *Collected Poems*, trans. by Barnard, O., Penguin Books, 1986, p.10

21  Ibid., p.168

22   Blake, W., *Complete Writings*, Oxford University Press, 1972, p.154
23   von Goethe, J.W., in Zajonc, A., *Catching the Light*, Bantam Books, 1993
24   Yeats, W.B., *The Collected Poems*, Macmillan and Co. Ltd., 1961, p.104
25   Fenollosa, E., *The Chinese Written Character as a Medium for Poetry*, City Lights Books, 1986
26   Sinclair, M., in Jones, P., (ed.) *Imagist Poetry*, Penguin Books, 1972, p.32
27   Pound, E., *Selected Poems*, Faber and Faber, 1959, p.127
28   Ibid., p.129
29   Li Po, Chinese poet, 701-762 A.D.
30   *The Holy Bible*, Authorized Version, Matthew, Ch.18, verse 3
31   Traherne, T., *Centuries*, The Faith Press, 1960, p.110
32   Lewis, R., (ed.) *Miracles*, Simon and Schuster, 1966, p.31 and p.55
33   Blake, W., *Collected Writings*, Oxford University Press, 1972, p.111
34   Rousseau, J.J., *A Discourse on the Origin of Inequality*, 1754
35   Wordsworth, W., in Kermode, F., and Hollander, J., (ed.) *The Oxford Anthology of English Literature, vol. 2*, Oxford University Press, 1973, p.609
36   Wordsworth, D., in Knight, W., (ed.) *The Journals of Dorothy Wordsworth*, Macmillan & Co., 1925
37   Wordsworth, W., in Kermode, F., and Hollander, J., (ed.) *The Oxford Anthology of English Literature, vol. 2*, Oxford University Press, 1973, p.174
38   Ibid., p.608
39   Matthews, P., in Angwin, R., (ed.) *Writing the Bright Moment*, Fire in the Head, 2005, p.72 (earlier version of this exercise)

# Earth, Water, Air and Fire

*We turn our attention to the four elements, Earth, Water, Air and Fire, and to how they manifest in our surroundings. Direct observation and memories of encounters with these elements are taken as a basis for writing. The elements are, however, more than states of matter. As qualities they can be found both in the many gestures of the natural world and in human temperament. Furthermore, their dynamics are observable in how we move, speak and write. These we practise here, asking how each element in turn can lend its quality to our writing. We close with a diagram in which these four qualities are shown to stand as an imaginative gateway between inner and outer worlds.*

A few miles east of Forest Row, into Kent, is the old house of 'Penshurst', which inspired Ben Jonson to write his poem 'To Penshurst', an excellent example of words in place. This is how it begins:

> Thou art not, Penshurst, built to envious show
> Thou joy'st in better markes, of soyle, of ayre,
> Of wood, of water: therein thou art faire.
> Thou hast thy walkes for health, as well as sport:
> Thy Mount, to which the Dryads doe resort...[1]

– a place, it seems, where Earth, Air, Water (Fire is not mentioned) and their attendant elemental beings are working together to create the harmonious dwelling that Ben Jonson so appreciated. These four elements offer a first way in to an apprehension of what speaks through the gestures of a place.

## Earth

Even stones have a love; a love that seeks the ground.[2]

*Meister Eckhardt*

To begin the week I placed a large black and white flint stone on the red carpet at the centre of our circle of chairs. I had it in mind that at the very end of our work together we would visit the chalk cliffs of 'The Seven Sisters', near Eastbourne, where this stone came from. For now, however, here it was – a thing starkly before us and out of context. What more fundamental experience of human inwardness meeting physical outwardness could there be than this, where I meet Stone? And the question with which we ended the previous section returns: how close up to a thing can we get with our consciousness and our language?

### Observing stone

At first we did not use language at all, but sat down to draw it using pastels on black paper. To produce great art was not the point. We took the act of drawing as a help to focus our attention, interest, appreciation, gratitude; eventually our love, perhaps. Only after that did we attempt to:

X 14. a) **Name it, noun it:** Stone. Rock. Stein… **in our various languages.**

b) **Write down the adjectives that belong to it:** Secure. Stable. Ancient. Curvaceous. Cold. Unmoving. Constant. Hard. Old. Silent. Separate. Gravity-filled.

c) Write the adjectives and potential verbs that arose out of our response to it: Mysterious. Hoping. Present. Lost. Lonely. Glowing. Waiting. Confined.

Then after sharing them in the group we

d) Inscribed the words into our pictures, and hung them up on the wall.

Flint stones

## Moving earth

X 15. Having reflected on these qualities of 'Earth' you can now embody them in movement; in your walking; in a handshake; in the clarity of position that your bones allow; in the gravity and differentiation which are the essential qualities of this Earth mode.

## Pondering rock

**X 16.  Write a piece about a particular stone in front of you, letting language arise out of this basic elemental meeting. Explore how 'Earth' can lend its quality to your words:**

> The rock sits hard and grey on the red rug. It is curved, but not round. Difficult to move; harder to change. Inflexible, certainly. It is what it is and what it has been – for how long, no one knows. Does this rock grow tired of its constant solidity? Does it weary of being reliable and predictable? Is its strength also isolation? Is it longing to be a feather? A rock can't cry and a rock can't bleed. But I can. Can a rock love?
>
> *Christine Meyer*

Demosthenes, in Ancient Athens, went straight to the point by placing a stone under his tongue to cure his stammering, and eventually became a famous orator. We, at least, can let it inform our rhythms and consonants:

> Here is a stone. Cold to my touch. Grey and separate. I could name it slate. That might not name it right. Grey, with flecks of white. It must've been laid down layer upon layer in water. This is not water. This bit of earth has been wrenched away from its belonging. Now here it is. In a room. Being looked at. It is visible. Visibly dry. It is not me. I am less hard. I hide my inwardness. This stone, though, it hides nothing. It is everywhere itself. Its outside is its inside. This true thing. I am less true. Stones do not lie. They do not worry or hurry or intentionally hurt, though humans used to use them to deal with malefactors. They were killed by this just thing. This cold grey justice. Could I find mercy in this grey matter? Just; but it does not judge me. Confronting it I ask – do I ring true against

its sides? This ground. This fundament. I lie in bed sometimes and pray gravity take me. Let all that I try so hard to be fall into Gravitas. Into the ground where this stone comes from and calls home.

*PM*

Another step in the meeting of this otherness would be to:

**X 17. Address the stone directly:**

Hey, you there! Are you God? Is that why I hate you so much, you old Bruiser?

Only joking! Your friendly fist first knocked the daylights into me and I am grateful.

**X 18. Or to speak for it. This is the progression (from *it* to *you* to *I*) that we explored more thoroughly on pages 55-58.**

## Remembering stone

This initial bumping of heads against mineral might help call to mind your meetings with other remarkable stones: the lucky pebble in your pocket? A chunk of the Berlin wall kept on the mantelpiece? The rock in the stream where your best thoughts come to you? Perhaps you remember the childhood excitement of digging up shards of pottery in the garden. And what about the pretty stones and shells, 'as small as a world and as large as alone',[3] that appear so miraculously on the tide line?

**X 19. You can elaborate such memories in writing. Was there a secret place, for instance, that provided a ground for you in childhood?**

## Stones in the landscape

Pix-in-Stones

Across the way the sculpture students are chipping and hammering as we scratch and sigh over our notebooks. Our task has been to give a voice to stone. Their final project is to place a sculpture in the college grounds in such a way that it interprets and articulates some gesture hidden within the landscape.

Certainly I experience the outcrops of sandstone in the fields above Emerson College as a sign or signature of this locality. There used to be a notice up there pinned to a beech tree saying Pix-in-Stones, obviously an earlier form of the name, Pixton, which is found across this hillside. My more sensible colleagues claim that 'Pix' refers to the picks of the miners who in Roman times dug iron here (hence Minepits Wood at the top of Tablehurst Farm). But there, too, you can find Pooks Hill, which allows me to think that 'Pix' might actually refer to the pixies that miners used to meet while working. Let me risk the 'silliness' of it, then, and say that this is pixy country.

In rhymen te tooky
The lib libs did gronder
Twas mockle mane spooky
A wib wib asunder.

Hey bey! See the tentacks
With lib libs a playing
Floster lip google pip
Flippers displaying!

Oh lalla, dip and dap
Gurgles and happy flap
Tentacks a ten a pack
Lib libs of mighty mack!

A rollin and zippering
In rhymen tel tooky
A lighten and lickitin
Twas mockle mane spooky!

*Carolina Read*

Rudolf Steiner, in fact, treated the nature spirits with utmost respect, 'gnomes' being the name he used for those who care for the roots, the Earth element.[4] We will meet them later as the Seven Dwarves who dig for gold and copper in the mountains (see p.198).

A more detailed study of 'Earth' would have to include a consideration of the different minerals and crystals, but that is beyond both the scope of this book and my expertise.

# *Water*

Who showed you the path of the poets?
The fountain and the stream of the antique song.[5]

F.G. Lorca

The River Medway

## Observing water

If you are lucky (or live in England) nature will provide you with a
rainy day to help you observe this element and to name what you
hear and see – the rhythm of it on the roof; the rounding and
running and merging of its drops as they roll down the windows;
the gurgle of water in the pipes; the many circles continually
forming and fading in the puddles; the gleam on the pine tree; the
rainbow if you are very lucky.

## Moving water

X 20.   We can walk as water, all gravity and flow. We can offer a watery handshake accompanied by a watery smile. Try clapping around the circle in a watery way; or throw a beanbag back and forth, becoming so at one with the movement that the beans do not rattle as you receive them into your hands. Water, it is clear, lends rhythm to movement, an endless flowing sentence of unpunctuated motion.

## Singing water

Here is a round we sang:

> The sound of the rain falling gently to the ground
> Brings peace and relief to a heart so full of care.

*Anon.*

## Reflecting on water

Once our bodies have remembered the 90% water that they are made of, we can name its many qualities – how it flows, spreads, rounds, reflects. It never ends. It serves. Is selfless. It is more a between than a thing. Water is not just sweet, of course, though tears of laughter are less salty than tears of sadness. Have you come across the research being done into how language can be imprinted into water, how water is harmonised or otherwise through a spoken word, or even a written one, and how it remembers each impulse that comes towards it?[6] One further step from there, and again we must regard it as an inhabited element, full of naiads, undines, nixies, mermaids (depending on which part of the world you come from) – some of them benign, some dangerous. How can we hold our ground in this realm of water? Odysseus in the presence of the Sirens' seductive sea song would have lost his ground had he not had himself bound to the mast to listen. As for the poet, John Keats, the epitaph that he made for himself: 'Here lies one whose name was writ on water',[7] is usually taken to be a sad reflection on the mutability of things, but I would say that it indicates his remarkable ability to hold identity within the fluid realm of imagination.

X 21.   Using water-colours, make a painting of the soul of water. What adjectives and verbs would you wish to write into its rippling surface?

X 22.   What is water? In trying to find a language to answer this, you could make use of 'perhaps' and 'maybe', and allow questions to well up as well as statements.

> What water is who knows? Maybe it likes to longs to wrap itself round about a stone. It is known to be selfless. Live long enough in water you become sleek and finned and find yourself mouthing words of no syllable and what you think is what you drink, tossing in a thirst which satisfies you even as it rages. Water. So simple minded. It remembers everything. Even the least stirring of a word troubles her countenance. I think I. What do I think? I think thirst came first, and then the water welled to it in service.
>
> *PM*

## Remembering water

X 23.   Write a personal anecdote arising out of an encounter with water, and in doing so let other qualities of water enter your use of language. Dissolve the punctuation, for instance, and permit the 'stream of consciousness' that so many writers in the 20th century experimented with:

I was drawn down to the seaside before dawn on a very calm morning like those mornings after a tremendous storm when the smooth, swaying surface of the silver water reflects the rose-orange glow of the cloudless sky above filled with the busy bodied gulls paying no heed to the beauty surrounding them and I, standing on the lone rock with the waves gently tickling the edges with their salty tongues and as I stood I marvelled at the splendour of this space of earth and wondered if it could be any more perfect than it was, which is the moment when my voice escaped into the stillness of the air and over the waves for a man once told me that seals love to hear high pitched songs, so I sang a song which had no name and I had never heard it before, yet I sang it over and over and still know it to this day, and as I stood filled with a great tide of emotion, there directly in front of my rock emerged a beautiful, sleek glossy head with dark, soulful eyes of glass gazing upon me without a blink, as I stood singing my mysterious song from the depths of my soul to this graceful water creature...

*Kira Orsak*

Rhythmic refrain is also something with which water can inform our words and phrases:

**Wayward Father**
The Golden Gate bridge is red.
From out at sea it's the red
getting caught up in the light
that attracts all sailors home.

When my father left to sail the world
his three daughters ran
to the bridge's middle
and showered his boat with flowers.

Our father set sail forever;
forever he said he'd sail the waters
or until he found his grail.

A sailor believes
the grail's at sea,
yet he drinks it dry on the seashore.

A song of a drunken sailor
has been eternally archetyped the sea.
Something of a wayward father
has me searching the bridges in water.

He is in rhythmic love with the ocean's freedom
pulsing in freedom
pulsing
yearning
yearning for the bridge to be golden
and for the sailor to reach his homeland.

*AD*

## Flow forms

At Emerson College we have a whole department, the Virbela Institute, devoted to the study and care of water. My colleague, John Wilkes, invented 'Flow Forms' in which the elements of earth and water come together in an artistic relationship. He gave me this brief statement about his work:

We are embedded within, surrounded by, and dependent upon rhythms of all kinds and yet they remain a mystery. Life and rhythm are indeed one. Water is the most sensitive carrier and mediator of rhythm. George Adams during the mid years of the last century was concerned with the influences particular

71

A Flow Form

surfaces might have upon water. These so-called path-curve surfaces are intimately involved with generative forms such as buds, cones and eggs that occur in a natural healthy context. Due to extensive morphological studies the question which attracted my attention in 1970 could be expressed as follows:

'Would it be possible to create for streaming water a vessel or indeed an "organ" which would enable it to manifest its potential for order and metamorphosis?'

As a result of my experiments it became gradually clear that rhythms are the result of resistance rather than some kind of mechanical process. The resulting Flowform Method which demonstrates a rhythmical lemniscatory process, made evident the close relationship between surface and rhythm. It immediately became possible to show that path-curve, combined with rhythms, could be investigated regarding their influence upon the quality of water when correct proportions were made available. The redeeming of life-supporting energy in water is with increasing intensity the subject of our investigations at the Institute.

*John Wilkes*

What I know is that here, at the back of Pixton House, water flows through a sculpted form and in that meeting a pulse arises in the water, a rhythm. It must be that flow and form are so subtly adjusted that the pulse arises; and now as I write about it I realise that my pen too is a meeting of form and flow – the blue ink pulses onto the paper, making blue sentences that have never been written before. Between moment and moment beside this fountain I give myself to the rhythm of what means to flows through me.

## *Air*

Wild air, world-mothering air.[8]

*Gerard Manley Hopkins*

### Observing air

In anticipation of this day I brought a pot of bubbles into the room. Someone else brought a feather. She stood on a chair and dropped it, and we watched it falling. Really, however, we did not have to import an airy experience. It was all around us. The polythene sheets covering the windows of our hut were rattling in the wind, and the roaring in the lime tree outside kept snatching our thoughts away – a feeling that some bigger event was going on out there above our heads, and that we were small beings in the path of it.

X 24.   **Give your full attention to the state of the air around you, and try to find words that name its particular qualities and activities:** e.g. Transparent. Everywhere and nowhere. Ungraspable. Sudden. Momentary. Transient. Light. Sprightly. Homeless. Mournful. Laughing.

## Moving air

Sometimes we meet people who carry an air about them, and, walking lightly on our toes and with nose turned upwards, we can join their company:

X 25.   **Try clapping around the circle again, this time as though trying to catch some invisible butterfly as it passes. Or you can blow kisses around the circle, throw beanbags to each other as though they were kisses, butterflies, bubbles. If the beanbag is then laid aside you can still keep throwing, making the weight, speed and direction of your intention visible. Then, each in turn, you can write your signatures large into the air and watch the tempo, flow and flight of your moving hands.**

## Musing on air

The wind: nobody sees it; only the results of it – how it carries fragrance, makes the leaves tremble. Leaves are tongues almost, each tree interpreting the air according to its nature, each breath of wind allowing ash, birch, beech to show their proper signatures. Ancient bards mused under the oak trees, believing the rustling of the leaves to be filled with rumours of divinity. More recently Percy Bysshe Shelley (a Sussex poet, born in Horsham), called out to the spirit in the wind: 'Make me thy lyre, even as the Forest is',[9] yet another example of a longing for a renewed 'participation' in the world process. Elsewhere (as Owen Barfield is keen to point out[10]) Shelley develops the concept of such a human harp more closely:

> Man is an instrument over which a series of external and internal impressions are driven, like the alternations of an ever-changing wind over an aeolian lyre, which move it by their motion to ever-changing melody. But there is a principle within the human being... which acts otherwise than in the lyre, and produces not melody alone, but harmony, by an internal adjustment of the sounds or motions thus excited to the impressions which excite them.[11]

You can hardly be a Romantic poet without once in your life wishing to be such a harp for the wind to play Aires upon. A feather for a pen might also help. We modern writers have our fountain pens, ballpoint pens, word-processors, and could not do without them, yet a part of me does regret that the quill (so open to the air where 'smalle fowles maken melodie'[12]) is out of fashion. The thought of it, if not the thing, can still accompany us in our writing.

## Winged words

*Earth* and *water* are obvious presences among the many activities at Emerson College, providing as they do the substance for those who work with the plastic arts. Now I am wondering how the element of *Air* declares itself here and, yes, it is all around us in the sung or spoken words that continually resound through our classrooms, or in evening gatherings and performances. Our lecturers 'wing it' rather than reading prepared papers and, at our weekly meetings of the whole college, students take courage to tell stories, recite poems, or speak about what is uppermost in their hearts and minds. Occasionally a fear grips me that this Emerson College that I have devoted my working life to might be some sort of backwater in the stream of contemporary life; but when I experience the paucity of language used in everyday commercial transactions, or even in some poetry readings that I attend, I come away with the conviction that the culture of living speech that we nurture here is a vital antidote to the strangled language that our times of information technology tend to produce. How can I say all this without sounding hopelessly arrogant and out of touch? If no one else, Homer, who so loved the winged word carried freely upon the breath, will have to be my surety in this.

*Air*, then, is that pole of language (see p.37) that manifests as fullness of expression. It howls in vowels. *Ha Ha*: one long in-breath followed by several short out-breaths. *Boo Hoo*: many short in-breaths following by a long moan breathing out.

## X 26. What is air? Yet again, in characterising the element, explore how the basic acts and rhythms named above can shape your language:

The grass tall bends and flings its wild sheaths to each point. The fence too now seems wild – it shines with wet all through its hard old tree stuff, makes homes for long deep cracks and short round rain pools. It sticks up and out the ground as if some man would say 'I'm here, you're there', but still it lives in earth. Up some more tall plants we call trees bend back and forth whip and slash and then stand still. But soon from now they sure will spill down once more and up a thrill so that my head turns round its will and looks still more to the air to find the place from where this rush of wind finds its store. All I see is air more breath and howl and shout and scream like in a bad night that I dream. The high tall trees stand stout and firm wet twigs and stems shake crash and squirm whilst all the air tries to climb through one tight hole. The smell of life blows through my face and yet is kind to this same place where I am left alone to stand.

*Ben Fairlight*

The use of one-syllable words that we practised earlier seems appropriate here (see p.49).

And here are some more lines from 'The Blessed Virgin Compared to the Air we Breathe', by Gerard Manley Hopkins:

> Again, look overhead
> How air is azured;
> Oh how! Nay do but stand
> Where you can lift your hand
> Skywards: rich, rich it laps
> Round the four fingergaps...[13]

## Remembering air

Such a task is, of course, best done in the presence or remembrance of the element. No need to stay stuck in the classroom. Go out and watch how the invisible movements of Air are interpreted through trees, birds, clouds, flags, paper bags rolling over and over, the quick footprint of wind over puddles; and then upon return let them inform your writing.

On the night of 16 October 1987, the Great Storm struck the South of England. Michael Fish, the BBC weatherman, had famously declared that no such thing was on its way, but when we woke in the morning there were trees every fifty yards lying across the streets of Forest Row. Neighbours who had kept to themselves for years began to talk to each other. The telephones were down, but the air between us rang with stories – that some people in Ashdown Road had moved out of their caravan just minutes before a tree came crashing down on it; that this was not merely storm, but meaningful – a language for the spirit; a message for the nation: Wake up to the forces you unleash when you interfere with nature.

X 27. **Write your own personal anecdotes of such encounters.**

## Inspiration

This airy element actually moves us, beyond the imaginative, into the realm of 'inspiration', a word that implies some breathing-in from elsewhere before our responding exclamation comes. No need to wait for some child on a cloud to appear (see p.50), although cloud-watching is indeed a rich source of images. Inspiration can be practised:

X 28. **Throw into a basket some of the words and phrases that arose when you imagined air together. Stir them with a feather. Breathe on them. Shake them gently. Well, don't be too serious about it. This is ritual play – to dedicate a crazy cornucopia of words to the ninefold blindfold Muses. Once the spell's wound up you can take whatever you need (whenever) from the basket, using what comes to you to write some airy pieces, full of praise and exuberance. Fullness of expression is not the only ideal at work in this airy mode; beauty is another:**

What a lot of names the wind has: Petal-Thief. Laugh-With-No-Mouth. Loosener-of Old-Hinges. There is a secret wind, they say, which, on the day appointed, moves over the wheatfield. Sometimes I have heard it called: He-Who-Without-Permission-Rushes-In-Everywhere. Oh, I don't know. It might be a Lady. Terror-And-Comfort-In-One – that's what I call it. If it named itself it might mouth something gusty like Soul-Of-All-Beings-Dancing-In-Spirals. Push-Through-To-Open. Rush-And-Rage-Open – that's what I call it. You don't know the wind, but the wind knows where to find you. First it roars in the Oak trees; then your shirt on the clothesline suddenly dances.

*PM: a collage of lines received from the group*

X 29. **If you have space enough, and a trained supervisor, you can have a go at throwing the discus.** The Ancient Greeks wrote spiral messages on theirs, throwing wish and supplication along with the material stuff. It is possible to throw a frisbee with something of that same quality.

## Fire

Thunderbolt steers all things.[14]

*Heraclitus*

### Observing fire

Who invented candles? I don't know. Whoever it was, I am grateful to them. I like to have candles in my classroom. Not as holy things. Just candles. Yet, being both beautiful and useful, they do provide the ideal opportunity for us to practise imagination even as we are observing them:

Here is a candle. Fire is our concern this morning, but we soon notice that this object (the result of someone's practical imagination) is actually four elements in one. Wick and wax, represent Earth, holding a small watery pool at the top. Then comes the uprush of air into the cone of blue; then the flame itself, held steady in its form yet ever-changing in its substance. Hot air rises; it rises to where it belongs. What else do we know about candles? Van Gogh put his hand in one to impress his girlfriend. More impressive, though, is to blow the candle out, put a match to the rising smoke and watch as the flame travels down the spume to settle on the wick again. Science and magic in one – an outer signature of some deeply inward momentum. She would have loved him for it.

## Moving fire

**X 30.  Move the qualities of fire.** If you ask someone to walk across the room in such a way they will certainly do so with a strong intention of going somewhere. If you ask someone to throw a beanbag with that quality, they will surely throw it over-arm at you, and it is likely that a slight feeling of aggression will accompany it. You can harness that energy by throwing a tennis ball over-arm, one bounce, across the circle, having carefully chosen your aim before doing so. A true aim. It is a small training of the will, preparing for a deed, and then accomplishing it. Fire experienced in movement has levity to it, and a forming individualising power, though when people gather round the fire to share their stories its social gesture is also very apparent.

**Spanish Dancer**
Just as a sulphur match ignites
and not yet steadying into flame
first spurts a quiver of white tongues: her dance
bursts instantaneous into life
as watchers startle from their dream.

And suddenly she's wholly flame and clear.

With just a glance she sets fire to her hair
and spins with perfect poise her dress
to incandescence – a flare
from which her shivering arms snake out
and stretch their glittering nakedness.

And then: as if she found the fire too tight,
she gathers it all together, casts it down

indignantly, with arrogant disdain
and looks upon the ground: it's spitting there,
and will not die back quietly or submit.
Yet sure of triumph, wearing now a sweet
smile of greeting she lifts up her face
and stamps it out with quick, small, certain feet.[15]

*Rainer Maria Rilke*

## Seizing the fire

**X 31.  The gesture of fire can be explored further (if you have trained supervision) through the activity of spear-throwing.**

It is not distance, however, that I look for, but that moment of beauty when the physical content of the spear coincides with the form of the parabola it is moving through and makes it visible. The equivalent in language of this shaking-of-spears would be to:

**X 32.  Create a poem in a new language in which, through its sounds and dynamics, we hear the Firebird singing. You can let a few known words float in if they want to:**

Traff lickiti plaff
Taf tiffle blim nimbleshak
Shish ashafish nash nizzel
Ziggabrazaggabik.[16]

This, then, will give us a clue of qualities to look for when we come back into conceptual language. Blake's famous poem, 'The Tyger' (see p.155), provides a good example – question after question (enhanced by an insistent heart-beat) in fiery dynamic. Such repetition always was the language of magic – to kindle the fire of will and change the world.

Although the poem is not about fire, the qualities of the element are interpreted through its manifestation as Tiger, and on that account we will allow it to be the spark here for our imaginings. Clearly the poet has an ambivalent attitude – is this fire worthy of awe and respect, or is it dangerous and destructive? On the one hand he alludes to mythological figures – Icarus (who aspired on wings, too close to the sun), and Prometheus (who seized fire from the gods, bringing it to earth for the creative use of human beings). This creative possibility of fire we will meet again in the Whitsun story (see p.185) which describes a divine spark coming down upon the brow of each one present. On the other hand, the poem strongly evokes the chains and furnaces of the industrial revolution, which Blake was inclined to condemn as satanic rather than divine activity.

**X 33. What is fire? This dual aspect of fire, and its ungraspable nature, finds appropriate expression in the following fragment:**

Fire will not look at itself. More than twice fire has thrown its vanity to the river. Collector of hallways, gatherer of banisters and the ceiling down. Fire is the one handed seducer. Fire, I watch you with my arms tied. Fire, you make me full. Do not call me mother. I call you – what I don't know. Fire is raptor. I am reaching for the hands of the fallen brothers. Fire is falcon in the mouth. What do you care of the names I give you. Fire is forgiveness. What do you see in my judge's robes? I am reaching for the hands of the fallen brothers. I am listening like a thief in the doorways of houses. Tell me what it means to fall and not stand straight again. Fire is hold up. Fire is gunpoint. Fire is blow.

*EW*

**X 34.** **The word equivalent to thunderbolts and spear-throwing is the diamond shaped poem (one word, two words, three words, two words, one word), starting with a commanding verb.**

Don't
neglect, candle,
to hold your
true name
steady

May
lightning strike
from under my
tongue when
talking

The second one here happens to become something of a magic charm. Very short poems with very short lines and sentences would also serve the purpose:

Van Gogh
met fire in apple trees.
He cut off his ear.
Nothing for him
stood still.
Cypress singed him.
Even the daisies here
would have scorched
his skin.
He shot himself.
The world
was too near.

                                                *PM*

## Remembering fire

**X 35.  It is time to pen some simple anecdotes arising out of your memories of fire. Here are some short random samples gathered from the group:**

> 'Hello, Mr. Carrot,' my young daughter said as I lit the fire in the grate, and I thought that's metaphor and personification in one – she must be a poet.

> I remember one November 5th when a spark got into the fireworks box and the Rockets and Catherine Wheels and Little Demons and Crackerjacks all went off at the same time.

> Sometimes when we had a bonfire we used to write our sins on pieces of paper and then throw them into the flames.

> I used to like throwing banana skins into the fire and hear them sing.

There are, of course, great fires that live in the world memory: for instance, the burning of the great temple at Ephesus. It could only have happened (so the story goes) because the tutelary goddess Artemis was absent, attending the birth of Alexander (the city of Alexandria was later named after him, and that, too, was the scene of a tragic fire when the great library went up in flames). Anyone familiar with major events of Rudolf Steiner's life would not fail to add to this list the burning of the first Goetheanum, the extraordinary wooden building that he designed as a house for the living Word. All these, it seems, were the work of arsonists – a misplaced use of our promethean energies.

## Fire of love

And now I am trying to think where *Fire* declares its presence in the immediate environment of Emerson College. We have a metalwork shop. We have a kiln. Most obviously, I suppose, we have a kitchen that provides lunch for the community throughout the year. Our biodynamic garden provides the vegetables, and then our cooks perform that everyday alchemy of putting Fire (the crowning element) below and, thereby, moving Earth towards Water, Water towards Air – I mean, they cook the potatoes. Hopefully, on another level, the enthusiasm of those who teach here activates a similar transmutation in the classroom.

Several times I have had cause to mention Francis Edmunds, the founder of this college – the fire in his eye, the way he started tapping his foot when, after listening to all the arguments, he knew what needed to be done. Fire was his element, and when a few months after he died the redwood tree in the garden was struck by lightning it was pretty clear to all of us that it was him trying to shake us out of our lethargy! Call this a myth if you like.

It is certainly another example of how people, misguidedly or not, feel that the elements act as a bridge between outer and inner worlds. Fire has always been regarded as the element in which physical substance gives way to the spiritual, or is the threshold between the two worlds. Hence Plotinus says that there are many beautiful things, and that the other elements partake of beauty, but only fire 'is beautiful in and by itself alone'.[17]

Here is a verse that Francis Edmunds composed for the lighting of the bonfire at the festival of St. John (see p.232):

> May the fire we light
> Consuming the branches of a living past
> Kindle to life in us
> The fire of love which creates anew.[18]

## *The Four Elements*

To end this week with the four elements, I have gathered the qualities and dynamics that we have been working with into my favourite diagram.

Central to it is the figure of Hermes/Mercury, god of thieves, merchants, healers, and poets. We have met him before (see p.26-7) in the left hand corner of Botticelli's *Primavera* – wings on his heels, and carrying the Caduceus – a staff with two snakes wound around it. If you find a coin in the street, it was he who dropped it; he lives by chance, in the present moment.

A version of this diagram appeared at the end of my earlier book, *Sing Me the Creation*. I have revised it now, bringing it into conformity with the old alchemical insights into the qualities of the four elements which are constantly at work, both in the outer world and in the human soul. Above the horizontal line are the levity-filled (uplifting) elements of Air and Fire; below it Water and Earth are given over to gravity. To the left of the vertical line

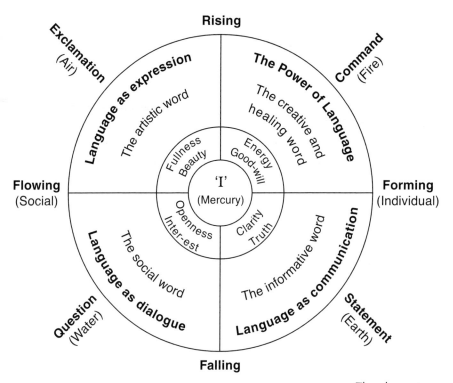

The elements

we find Air and Water with their mingling properties; to the right of it are the elements of Fire and Earth with their tendency to form and differentiate.

According to the early Greek philosopher, Empedocles, it is love and strife that activate these four powers.[19] The alchemists (those imaginative scientists of a former age) would add that Christ, the I Am, 'the true Mercury', stands at the centre, setting form and energy, gravity and levity against each other for destruction or weaving them together in fruitful interaction. W.B. Yeats (another lover of fourfold diagrams) bases his whole book, *A Vision* (which had its inception in Forest Row, see p.15), on this dynamic doctrine, and I am happy to follow his lead in this. My own version of this mandala of the elements points, on the one hand, to the spatial dynamics at the heart of grammar and on the other provides a language to help us articulate the qualities of nature's gestures and human movement.

X 36.   It would be good now to look back on the clapping, walking, throwing activities that we have done, and enact them all in relation to the four elements. The attempt to balance a rod on one finger provides a living experience of Mercury's Caduceus, holding an upright centre and identity within an environment of snaking energies.

## Invocation

X 37.   Invoke the muses of the four elements, calling down their particular blessings into your work as a writer:

I am grateful to the Muse of Water, for the renewal of deep springs, the music and motion of riverbank and wave break, for the thrill of the sudden strong current, and the bliss of boundaries dissolving in the flow. And to the Fire for its energy flashing, the sparks' unexpectedness, brightness in the dark, the fiery crystals that both illuminate and gather light about them. From Fire, though, I would ask for courage to hold and shape that energy, to sustain a steady heat, to let my words burn clear.

Muse of Earth, I would like to ask you for strength of form. Both fire and water tend to blur distinctions, to leap over boundaries, to change shape so fast it's dizzying. But to write in forms as clear, precise, and subtle as a leaf? To have a bold design, like tiger stripes. To be as spare as bone. To grasp the whole as surely as the part. And to know when a thing is ripe – and to let go – for that I need your art. And more: your stability and quiet (Water and Air are rarely still). To stay in one place. To know the roots as well as the fluttering leaves. To grow deep and slow as your heartbeat. To hear the silence in between. For that I need your patience, Muse of Earth.

And Air, your inspiration not least. Water murmurs and sings. Fire flashes, rustles, cracks, ignites. But you carry the breath of the cosmos. You are so big you scare me most of all. I can't grasp you, but you are not for grasping. You speak of the heights and of emptiness. You speak of God. What can I ask of you?

*Karen Anderson*

Here is a verse from Celtic sources in which the qualities of the elements are invoked as blessings:

Deep peace of the running wave to you
Deep peace of the flowing air to you
Deep peace of the shining stars to you
Deep peace of the quiet earth to you.[20]

## The shadows of imagination

No book dedicated to imagination can go without some mention of Samuel Taylor Coleridge. 'Imagination', he said, 'is the repetition in the finite mind of the eternal act of creation in the infinite I AM',[21] – a definition that I am happy to add to our growing list. His angle on it, however, was quite different from that of his friend, William Wordsworth:

It was agreed that my endeavours should be directed to persons and characters supernatural, or at least Romantic; yet so as to transfer from our inward nature a human interest and a semblance of truth sufficient to procure for these shadows of imagination that willing suspension of disbelief for the moment, which constitutes poetic faith. Mr. Wordsworth, on the other hand, was to propose to himself as object, to give the charm of novelty to things of everyday, and to excite a feeling analogous to the supernatural, by awakening the mind's attention to the lethargy of custom, and directing it to the loveliness and the wonders of the world before us.[22]

We will meet those persons and characters supernatural more fully when we come to fairy tales (see p.195) but before we proceed with our initial Wordsworthian approach, we do need (with Coleridge's help) to poke our noses briefly through the gates of their Secret Garden:

### Kubla Khan

In Xanadu did Kubla Khan
A stately pleasure dome decree:
Where Alph, the sacred river, ran
Through caverns measureless to man
Down to a sunless sea.
So twice five miles of fertile ground
With walls and towers were girdled round:
And there were gardens bright with sinuous rills,
Where blossomed many an incense-bearing tree;
And here were forests ancient as the hills,
Enfolding sunny spots of greenery.

But oh! That deep romantic chasm which slanted
Down the green hill athwart a cedarn cover!
A savage place! As holy and enchanted
As e'er beneath a waning moon was haunted
By woman wailing for her demon-lover!
And from this chasm, with ceaseless turmoil seething,

As if this earth in fast thick pants were breathing,
A mighty fountain momently was forced:
Amid whose swift half-intermitted burst
Huge fragments vaulted like rebounding hail,
Or chaffy grain beneath the thresher's flail:
And 'mid these dancing rocks at once and ever
It flung up momently the sacred river.
Five miles meandering with a mazy motion
Through wood and dale the sacred river ran,
Then reached the caverns measureless to man,
And sank in tumult to a lifeless ocean:
And 'mid this tumult Kubla heard from far
Ancestral voices prophesying war!
The shadow of the dome of pleasure
Floated midway on the waves;
Where was heard the mingled measure
From the fountain and the caves.
It was a miracle of rare device,
A sunny pleasure dome with caves of ice.

A damsel with a dulcimer
In a vision once I saw:
It was an Abyssinian maid,
And on her dulcimer she played,
Singing of Mount Abora.
Could I revive within me
Her symphony and song,
To such a deep delight 'twould win me,
That with music loud and long,
I would build that dome in air,
That sunny dome! Those caves of ice!
And all who heard should see them there,
And all should cry, Beware! Beware!

His flashing eyes, his floating hair!
Weave a circle round him thrice,
And close your eyes with holy dread,
For he on honey-dew hath fed,
And drunk the milk of Paradise.[23]

In his 'Preface' to the poem (not included here) Samuel Taylor Coleridge claims to have composed it 'in a profound sleep, at least of the external senses', so we should not be surprised to find that the geography of Kubla's garden does not stand still. After a while of testing our brains against the text we found we could actually make more sense of its dynamics through our fingertips:

**X 38. Take a large sheet of paper and, in unspoken collaboration with a partner, make a pastel drawing of the images and dynamics of the poem.**

Reflecting later upon the movements and colours that our hands had traced, we saw that we had mapped, without really meaning to, our present theme of opposites and elements, and that creativity itself is the real subject of the piece.

In that same 'Preface', Coleridge (in extreme contrast to the fiery confidence he ends with) apologises for the poem, declaring that he publishes it as a 'psychological curiosity' rather than for any literary merit it might have. No need for the apology, though many a time in my writing groups apology comes before the sharing of a poem just created; it denotes an honouring of the creative threshold. But the psychologists among us can, indeed, have a hay-day with this poem in attempting to understand the artistic mind. The contrast between the sunny measured garden and 'the caverns measureless to man', for instance, with Alph, the sacred river, meandering between them – this mirrors exactly the tension that the poet lived with. In his daytime guise he considered himself to be a rational Christian gentleman. Night after night, however, often in nightmare form, he met demonic females who tempted him to things that Christian philosophers don't usually admit to the thinking of. She even told him her name – Ebon Ebon Thalud.[24] What on earth or elsewhere could that be about? 'Ebony', perhaps. Or, spell her backwards, and her name is 'No be'. As for Thalud – 'Thelism' is the philosophy of Will. A dark female will, twice over (we will get a glimpse of her again in the looking glass of Snow White's wicked stepmother, see p.240). And yet, if those energies are not denied, she may well turn playful, 'Thalia' being the Muse of Comedy.

Coleridge, like others of the Romantics, was intrigued by the underside of things. At the same time, he feared it. He feared his own sexuality, perhaps. It certainly asserts itself in the poem with orgasmic force – 'the mighty fountain' with its 'swift half-intermitted burst'. Far from being a description of an outer landscape, the whole poem can be understood in terms of physiological process. I include it here because we need to know that in crossing that inner threshold we encounter our selves, possibly not as 'the fairest of them all', but with all our hang-ups and obsessions intertwined. If on the path of imagination we avoid that meeting, then the truth and untruth of what we see there is indistinguishable. Not that I wish to reduce this poem to a private case study. It is, in fact, one of the great visionary poems in our literature – an influx from some immeasurable realm that the poet touched into between sleep and waking. This river Alph – flowing from dark to light then dark again – images the creative process. Most importantly for my theme of *Words in Place*, it implies that what lives in our seemingly abstract alphabet is not just hooked on to things but streams somehow within the green heart of nature. We can remember this as we turn now to see how closely we can touch with our words the world of plants.

# *Notes*

[1] Jonson, B., *The Poems of Ben Jonson*, Routledge and Kegan Paul, 1962, p.76

[2] Meister Eckhardt, source not traced

[3] cummings, e.e., *Selected Poems*, Penguin Books, 1960, p.170

[4] Steiner, R., *Man as Symphony of the Creative World*, Rudolf Steiner Press, 1979, p.120

[5] Lorca, F.G., *The Ballad of the Little Square*, trans. by Gili, J.L., Penguin Books, 1960, p.1

[6] Emoto, M., *The Hidden Messages in Water*, Beyond Words Publishing Inc., 2004

[7] Keats, J., Epitaph on his gravestone, Rome

[8] Manley Hopkins, G., *Poetry and Prose*, Penguin Books, 1998, p.80

[9] Shelley, P.B., 'Ode to the West Wind' in *The Complete Published Works Of Percy Bysshe Shelley*, Clarendon Press, 1972

[10] Barfield, O., *The Rediscovery of Meaning*, Wesleyon University Press, 1977, p.67

[11] Shelley, P.B., in *Poets on Poetry*, Collier Books, 1962, p.180

[12] Chaucer, G., The Prologue, *Canterbury Tales*

[13] Manley Hopkins, G., *Poetry and Prose*, Penguin Books, 1998

[14] Kirk, G.S., Raven, J. E. and Schofield, M., *The Presocratic Philosophers*, Cambridge University Press, 1955

[15] Rilke, R.M., *Neue Gedichte*, trans. by Barton, M.

[16] Matthews, P., *Sing Me the Creation*, Hawthorn Press, 1994, p.107

[17] Plotinus, *Plotinus on the Beautiful, First Ennead*, The Shakespeare Head Press, 1914, p.16

[18] Edmunds, L.F., *Circles*, Emerson College, 1990

[19] Empedocles, 'On Nature', in Wright, M. R., *Empedocles: The Extant Framents*, Yale University Press, 1981

[20] Celtic Blessing, from the Gaelic

[21] Coleridge, S.T., *Biographia Literaria*, J.M. Dent & Co., 1906, Ch.13

[22] Ibid., Ch.14

[23] Coleridge, S.T., *Poetical Works*, Oxford University Press, 1973, p.295

[24] Holmes, R., *Coleridge: Early Visions*, Hodder and Stoughton, 1989, p.293

# Turning a New Leaf

*Having explored the four elements as qualities of movement and language, we now extend this into modes of encountering the world of plants, concentrating first upon the mode of Earth (the most detached and formed), and of Water (in which we attend to movement and relationship). In grammar these manifest as statement and question. The writing that arises may seem to lack poetry at first, but if our words are to have truth in them as well as beauty then this more scientific mode provides a necessary ground and discipline for the imagination.*

As mentioned at the very beginning of this book, we do have 'forests ancient as the hills' around Emerson College (like Kubla Khan), but no 'Romantic chasms', I'm afraid, except the usual ones between people. The garden around Pixton House is cultivated land, with a Ha-Ha at the bottom of it, to help us see the peasants working in the distance, I suppose, but not to smell them. That, anyway, is how it used to be; but since the college moved here the wild has been allowed to encroach a little (the mole tunnels under the front lawn are 'measureless to man', indeed), and our own imaginings have moved out a little, shaping a flowering garden that is deeply supportive of the studies. The St. John Garden where the ashes of dead colleagues are laid is truly a place where 'ancestral voices' can speak if you stand quiet enough. As for 'sinuous rills', the Flow Form in the pond (which is designed, by the way, to pulse in 'intermitted bursts') will have to serve as that.

## *Plant and stone*

To begin the week, I placed our flint stone at the centre of the circle again, and a flowering plant beside it. We then began to characterise the plant through how it differed from the stone. If, for instance, you break a stone in half it becomes two stones; do the same to a daffodil and it becomes two parts of a dead one. What do we learn from that? That it is more highly differentiated than a stone; more organised. It is alive. It grows; needs nourishment from all the elements. It reproduces; breathes. It flows with sap. It even moves, but only in response to the moving sun. It dies, then comes again. It lives rhythmically in time. It takes no revenge upon those who trample it.

## *Getting engaged*

As a foundation for the project of these next two 'Weeks' you will need to choose a particular spot in the open air where a plant is growing and flowering. Don't go out with too determined an intent to find one. Walk, rather, with an open gaze (we practised this on our haiku hike, see p.33) and an open heart, and let the plant make the first advances. Once the engagement is confirmed, you can:

X 39.   **Describe the place you have chosen to someone else in the group. Describe how to get there. What drew you towards it? Who did you meet along the way? What is to be found there? What mood surrounded that place on your first visit? You could then bring it into writing:**

> **Hellebore (i):** Under a big pine tree with an elder bush at the foot, and hawthorn and cow parsley beside, I found it. It was right there beside the path leading out of the 'St. John Garden'.

Hellebores in light
old stone step
twisted roots
3 stones — a threshold
through the dark
archway
from St John's Garden

I felt the contrast of going through the dark yew archway like a threshold and then seeing Richard bending down and holding the purple flower in his hand as if he was showing it to me. When I first looked at the plant I thought the light green shooting leaves in the middle were comfrey, or some other plant; then I realised it was the new growth of this year, and, looking closer, I found that the flowers which hung down around it were from last year's leaves, coming from under the ground...

*Margaret Shillan*

We will be following the Hellebore (in both word and image) through various modes of meeting, interspersing pieces written in response to other members of the plant kingdom:

X 40.  **This first impression could also be conveyed through a painting or pastel drawing, more mood map than picture.** It is important to gather a sense for the whole before we go into details.

X 41.  **Write now, out of such a sense of wholeness for your plant in its place, a fuller description (perhaps in the form of a letter to someone), including its mineral, plant, animal, and human environment, its relation to light and shade. How does it respond to the wind? Is it sheltered? What is the weather around that place?**

> **Campion:** If you walk down beyond the cultivated garden, that's where you will find it – in the beginning of the wildwood. There were a few of them, shining pink among the tangle of undergrowth. The stems of my plant do not stand up straight and tall, but straggle everywhere, caught among brambles. Somehow I don't want that. Yet I accept it. This morning as I was ambling towards my chosen corner I met Katie who said how 'clement' the weather was. And that is exactly the word for it – neither too hot nor too cold, but clement. It is not everyday that you can use the word 'clement'. So today I use it. Clement. Clement. Clement. My straggly pink campion (I think it is) shaking in the clement wind. Its long stem wanders and then kind of forgets where it has been, dies off, but then sends out another perfect stem from its side. It is dark there under the oak trees. Little pink flower in search of light...
>
> *PM*

The old haiku masters in Japan (as, indeed, many Asian people) never completely lose a sense of wholeness. Basho, it is true, professed to be troubled by poetry that is too subjective or objective. It was, however, relatively easy for him to meld those poles together in the act of meditation:

> Go to the Pine if you want to learn about the Pine or to the Bamboo if you want to learn about the Bamboo. And in doing so, you must leave your subjective preoccupation with yourself. Otherwise you impose yourself on the object and do not learn. Your poetry issues of its own accord when you and the object have become one – when you have plunged deep enough into the object to see something like a hidden glimmering there.
>
> However well phrased your poetry may be, if your feeling is not natural – if the object and you are separate – then your poetry is not true poetry but merely subjective counterfeit.[1]

It seems to me that he was still within what Owen Barfield calls 'original participation',[2] that state of consciousness which (before the Hebrews and the Greeks stepped away from it) held the whole of the ancient world in its motherly embrace (see p.20). We can certainly learn from the practice of haiku (where artistic and religious practice are still at one), but we in the western world have moved so far from home, that Basho's 'hidden glimmering' will need to be kindled again through conscious exercises that warm our thinking:

> Ah! From the soul itself must issue forth
> A light, a glory, a fair luminous cloud,
> Enveloping the Earth...[3]

Coleridge saw the question clearly, and suffered it all his life.

## 'New Eyes for Plants'

I cannot go further without acknowledging the work of Dr. Margaret Colquhoun, my occasional colleague. Her book, *New Eyes for Plants*,[4] that she created with Axel Ewald (another former colleague), has helped me grasp the potential of my own work. In that book drawing is the chosen medium of engagement, yet the value of what I am trying to say here regarding a poetic/scientific approach to the plant would be greatly enhanced through a reading of it. In the previous section we explored the properties of Earth, Water, Air and Fire as states of matter, and how they can be taken up into the qualities of our language. It was through Margaret, who got it from Jochen Bockemühl,[5] who was inspired by J.W. von Goethe, who admired Paracelsus,[6] that it first became clear to me that those elements are present as gestures in Root (Earth), Leaf (Water), Flower (Air), Fruit (Fire), and that they provide four modes whereby we can progressively perceive and know the inwardness of nature.

## Planting our feet

The first step of this project (after our attempt to sense the whole) is an acknowledgement of the 'onlooker' consciousness that we have arrived at in our time and culture:

X 42.  Draw the particulars of your plant. To do this it might be necessary to dig up a specimen. Measure it. Count its parts and learn their botanical names, then annotate your drawings with the results of your researches. If you bring other senses into play – touch, smell, taste – do bear in mind that some plants are poisonous. Finally, you can write a paragraph describing the plant in detail. This should be in the 'it' (Earth) mode that we practised earlier (p.55): exact sense perception. In grammar it appears as statement:

Fresh new growth of this year's leaves

Old leaves from last year lying on the ground

Flowers spring up the following year from bud under the ground

**Hellebore (ii):** It has sundry fair green leaves rising from the root, each of them standing about a handful high from the earth; each leaf is divided into seven, eight, or nine parts, dented in the middle of the leaf to the point sides, abiding green all the winter; about Christmas-time, if the weather be

101

anything temperate, the flowers appear upon foot-stalks, also consisting of five large, round, white leaves a-piece, which sometimes are purplish towards the edges, with many pale yellow thrumbs in the middle; the seeds are black, and in form long and round. The root consists of numberless blackish strings all united into one head. There is another species which grows in the woods, very like this, but only the leaves are smaller and narrower, and perish in the winter, which this does not.[7]

*Nicholas Culpeper*

When I first took up my work at Emerson College my poet friend, Paul Evans, had the impression that most of the poems by my early students were about trees (there are a lot of them round here), and how unfair to trees it is to use them as cosmic symbols without first honouring their outward prickly existence. Goethe would have agreed with him:

It makes a great difference whether the poet seeks the particular for the universal or beholds the universal in the particular. From the first procedure originates allegory, where the particular is considered only as an illustration, an example of the universal. The latter, however, is properly the nature of poetry; it expresses something particular without thinking of the universal or pointing to it. Whoever grasps this particular in a living way will simultaneously receive the universal too, without ever becoming aware of it, or realise it only later.[8]

It is not enough to visit your plant just once. Go to it every day, rain or shine. Note and sketch any changes in plant and mood and weather, and try to disentangle them from each other. You could call now upon your power of memory to retain those images, testing them again and again against the sense phenomena. They will gain in accuracy thereby, but become somewhat fixed in the process. Do you find it boring to keep doing this? Then take courage from what Goethe said: 'Every process in nature rightly observed wakens in us a new organ of cognition';[9] or from what I say:

**B**oredom, **O**nce **R**espected, **E**ventually **D**eepens **O**ur **M**inds.

*flowers hanging down becoming like leaves - greenish*

*fresh new leaves opening up like chalices*

*leaf flower seed pod all similar shape*

*leaf rosettes*

## Going with the flow

In this next stage of the work the fluid element of water lends its qualities to our engagement with the plant:

X 43.  **Visit someone else's plant and inter-view them about it. Ask them to do the same for you. Ask each other questions about it.** If you lend eyes to each other in this manner then the previously unnoticed details that you discover will rekindle your interest.

X 44. **Jot down the questions about your plant that arose during the interview, and then add more of your own. Take the various question words – what, where, when, why, which, how – as a way in:**

> **Hellebore (iii):** Is it a native plant? Where did it come from? Who brought it here – gardener or wind? What is the origin of its name? How old is this plant? When did the seedpods start to grow? How long before its petals fade? When did its new leaves start to grow?
>
> *Margaret Shillan*

Many of these questions are concerned with how the plant lives within the flow of time. In this watery mode another question that becomes important is how the plant lives in relationship to its environment:

> **Hellebore (iv):** I have discovered that the Hellebore plays a vital role in feeding the humble bumble bees and wood bees through the winter and spring. It is one of those plants which, having huge nectar pockets, like great mead chalices, bloom and produce masses of nectar when there is little else around to feed and maintain these creatures.
>
> *Richard Heys*

## Green grammar

Live long enough in the watery form of the question-mark, you might find your way into the flux of things and begin to ask why, for instance, do the leaves at the bottom of the stem differ from those at the top?

Here is a sequence of leaf-forms from a single plant which, while stylised, remains true to the natural order:

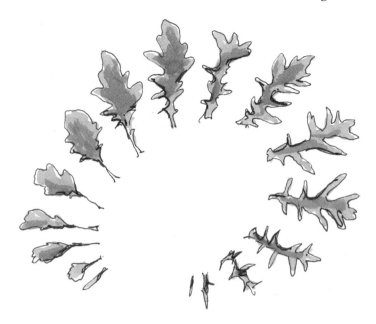

Sequence of leaf-forms

If we revert to our first (earthy) approach for a moment we can, through exact sense perception, take note of the single leaf-forms and commit them to memory. Such a practice is important, and yet it is as though you were reading the words and letters on this page without noticing that something is streaming invisibly through them to form this sentence that, hopefully, you have understood. But now:

X 45.  a)  Let your eye, in combination with your senses for movement and balance, move through the sequence backwards and forwards.

   b)  Make copies of this leaf sequence and then, having separated the individual leaves, ask a group of people (who have not seen the original) to arrange them in 'a satisfying order'.

Through such observation and thinking, and through a subtle attention to your breathing, you can learn to read the patterning intelligence at work in the plant and come to understand a little of what the poet, William Wordsworth, meant when he spoke of:

A motion and a spirit, that impels
All thinking things, all objects of all thought,
And rolls through all things.[10]

Scientists who have devoted their lives to this Goethean method of observation have recognised a fourfold grammar in the metamorphosis of the leaf patterns as they progress from bottom to top:

pointing         (Fire)
differentiating  (Air)
spreading        (Water)
stemming         (Earth)

You might say it is another example of a Flow Form – the sap rising, and a rhythm coming about in response to the resistances its meets along the way (see p.71).

My own abiding interest in the relationship of word and world has led me to connect these creative dynamics made visible in the leaves to the four archetypal acts that give life to language – of statement, question, exclamation and command.

X 46.  Embody in movement the manner in which the leaves of your plant (or even the whole plant) relate to these four dynamics.

X 47.  With these principles in mind, visit your particular plant and, having observed its leaves, make a careful drawing of

**how they manifest.** Different plants will emphasise them differently according to their nature (the hellebore that we are following, for instance, seems to be of a watery spreading nature), and even different specimens of the same plant may vary, depending upon how much water and light there is in their environment. In this way the signatures of plant and place start to reveal themselves.

X 48.  **Draw your plant from memory.** 'Only that which I can draw from memory I have truly understood',[11] said Goethe.

Hellebore: drawn from memory

Once that is done you can bring together the various drawings done by the group and note how the elemental gestures of rose, hellebore, campion etc. differ from one another. You might be able to make a mandala of them in relation to the diagram of the elements on p.87.

## Exact sensory imagining

All these exercises are preparation for the work that Goethe recommended of transforming mental images, inwardly following the metamorphosis of one form into another with the help of fantasy.

Fantasy, usually considered to be a subjective and unreliable thing ('deceiving elf', Keats might call it, see p.162), is hereby given an objective sensory basis, while the more static memory images are, in turn, quickened through its mobile power. According to Goethe, it is in the union of these polar faculties that a new organ of perception arises, 'exact sensory imagining', through which we can enter the time process of the plant and know it from the inside. Once practised with the leaf-sequence, this can be done with the whole life-cycle of your plant.

Goethe was not interested in formulating intellectual ideas about what he observed. 'Don't look for anything behind the phenomena,' he said, 'they themselves are the theory.' When his friend Schiller dismissed his claim of having discovered the *Urpflanze* (Archetypal Plant) by saying, 'That is no experience, that is an idea', Goethe famously replied: 'I am glad to have ideas without knowing it, and to see them with my own eyes.'[12] The fact that 'theory' and 'idea' both stem from a root meaning 'to see', points back to an earlier mode of consciousness which was able to see both meaning *and* things in the world.

Although (as we have seen, p.106) William Wordsworth in his first enthusiasm shared such certainties, he later fell away from them into a sense of loss for the 'splendour in the grass'[13] that he had known in childhood. Goethe, however, giving his full attention to the leaves in front of him, had no time for such sentiments, recovering through the practice of exact sensory imagining that early childhood state in which perception and thought are not yet polarised.

X 49.   **We end this section as we began, with questions, but this time addressing them directly to the plant:**

**Hellebore (v):** Why are your petals white and five? What are you trying to tell me through your winter flowering? Have you tapped into some special substance beneath the soil which makes you blush magenta? When your roots cure madness do they leave enough to understand you by?

*Margaret Shillan*

**Perriwinkle:** or Vinca Dubia – is that the name that Adam gave you? Since when did you live in the spot between the Red Studio and the fence? Why do you hide yourself among the other plants? Are you timid about the world? Do you live in secret? Why are the movements of your leaves so fluid? I wonder, too, where you get the dark purple colour of your flower, and why the shape of a star in your petals is so clear and awake. Do you have an intention, or are you just there, free? How do you feel living in the wild ground and making your way through the wildness of the grass? Are the bushes and dandelions friendly to you? And the bees? Do they visit you? Do you allow them to come into your pentagonal tiny cupola in the centre of your being? Is that where you gather the light from the sun?

*Nanda Lopes*

In this way we prepare an active inner space which can invoke the inspirations (the 'Aha' moments) that belong to the next stage of the process.

# *Notes*

1  Basho, M., *The Narrow Road to the Deep North*, Penguin Books, 1966, p.33

2  Barfield, O., *Saving the Appearances*, Wesleyan Press, 1989

3  Coleridge, S.T., 'Dejection: An Ode' in *Poetical Works*, Oxford University Press, 1973

4  Colquhoun, M., and Ewald, A., *New Eyes for Plants*, Hawthorn Press, 1996

5  Jochen Bockemühl worked in the Research Laboratory at the Goetheanum in Switzerland

6  Paracelsus, 1494-1541, Swiss Physician and Alchemist

7  Culpeper, N., *Culpeper's Complete Modern Herbal*, W. Foulsham and Co. Ltd., p.181

8  von Goethe, J.W., source not traced

9  von Goethe, J.W., *Man or Matter*, Ernst Lehrs, Faber and Faber, 1958, p.85

10  Wordsworth, W., *The Major Works*, Oxford World Classics, 2000, p.569

11  von Goethe, J.W., in *New Eyes for Plants*, Hawthorn Press, 1996, p.37

12  von Goethe, J.W., *Man or Matter*, Ernst Lehrs, Faber and Faber, 1958, p.104

13  Wordsworth, W., *The Major Works*, Oxford World Classics, 2000, p.569

# The Flowering Garden and our Responses to it

*Now that we have faithfully engaged in these modes of Earth and Water we can turn with confidence towards what Air and Fire invite us into. In language they manifest as exclamation and command, and in the I/You relationship which gives more scope for imagination and poetry. Through exercises in moving, drawing and writing the language of nature begins to reveal itself.*

To live in question regarding the difference between one thing and another is the beginning of a conscious cultivating of the imaginative faculty. I have learnt this particularly from Rudolf Steiner who, in his handbook for the cultivation of the inner life, *How to Know Higher Worlds*,[1] indicates the value of giving our attention first to a flourishing plant, then to a dying one, noting what is there before our eyes, then contemplating the subtle feelings and sensations that arise as we move between the two experiences. So often our emotional life swings uncontrollably between joy and woe, sympathy and antipathy, but through the practice described here the 'heart's affections'[2] (as John Keats called them) can be made *holy*, open to behold what is moving in the heart of Nature (see p.147).

# *Airing our views*

Someone deeply gifted in this (but without the ground under foot that we have worked for) was the 18th century poet, Christopher Smart, who was born in Shipbourne, forty miles downstream on the same River Medway that flows through Forest Row. Here is a fragment from 'Jubilate Agno', a poem that he wrote one line a day in the lunatic asylum to which he was committed for being too praiseful of God in public:

> For there is no height in which there are not flowers.
> For flowers have great virtues for all the senses.
> For the flower glorifies God and the root parries the adversary.
> For the flowers have their angels even the words of God's Creation.
> For the warp & woof of flowers are worked by perpetual moving spirits.
> For flowers are good both for the living and the dead.
> For there is a language of flowers.
> For there is a sound reasoning upon all flowers.
> For elegant phrases are nothing but flowers.
> For flowers are peculiarly the poetry of Christ.
> For flowers are medicinal.
> For flowers are musical in ocular harmony.
> For the right names of flowers are yet in heaven.
> God make gardners better nomenclators.[3]

Crazy though this may seem, we can understand why Dr. Samuel Johnson said he would prefer Kit Smart as praying partner to any of his more orthodox companions.[4] It is, actually, well worth contemplating each line in turn. The 'perpetual moving spirits' that he mentions are, no doubt, the elemental gnomes, undines, sylphs and salamanders that we have already had occasion to refer to. Rudolf Steiner says:

These elemental beings are all around us, begging us not to look at flowers so abstractly nor form such abstract images of them, but rather let our heart and mind enter into what lives as soul and spirit in the flowers, imploring us to break their spell of enchantment. Human life should really be engaged in continuously releasing from enchantment the elemental spirits imprisoned in minerals, plants and animals.[5]

As for flowers 'musical in ocular harmony', you only have to go to Sissinghurst with its colour-coded garden (about an hour's drive east of Emerson College) to witness that.

**X 50.  Now make your own version. Or you can pass a paper around the group, reading what came before and taking that as inspiration to add your own:**

For flowers are windows for the dead.
For flowers are beautiful without need for admirers.
For flowers have eyes and watch over our behaviour.
For flowers are neither clothed nor naked.
For flowers can be both beautiful and poisonous.
For some flowers have a dark heart and are dangerous to
  wayfarers.
For flowers lend their names to girls, but to boys more
  reluctantly.
For flowers have been found pressed between the pages of
  Deuteronomy.

## Fairest of them all

What, in all of nature, is the fairest of them all? It is the flower, surely. And our immediate response is to wonder at her beauty. But 'Beauty is not enough', says Edna St. Vincent Millay (see p.25). Perhaps it is only sentimental facets of ourselves that we are seeing; only what we want to see, not what's really 'out there'. Even Snow White with her innocent eye could not discern the poison in the pretty things and smiling faces that came to her window, and had to be three times tested before she could make true appraisal of what beauty is (see p.202 and pp.244-247). In something of the same way, through head, and heart, and moving limbs, we have been testing what it means to meet a flower.

**X 51. You can gather now much of what we have done into a more fulsome piece by composing a letter to your chosen plant:**

**Hello Hellebore (vi),**

Why do you flower at Christmas – even in the snow and cold? Is it to bring new hope to people? We call you Christmas Rose. Always, I thought you were a flower, but a wise woman told me that transformed leaves is what you really are! – from white or violet or palest, freshest green to a kind of grey-green – changing your colours as you get older. I know how that feels! Some people call you Lenten Rose; I am sure that is appropriate, flowering, as you do, before Easter, and then when your new leaves come it's like a kind of resurrection. That is what I felt when I first saw you. There you were, shooting up with huge energy, and I can well understand that they say you are strong medicine for cancer and madness and plague. It is hard to know you when so much of who you are is rooted deep underground, your flower/leaves down there shooting bright magenta; and you even have little buds waiting in the dark for next year's sprouting. So many of your secrets are still hidden from me, Hellebore, but thank you for taking me to this place of mystery!

*Margaret Shillan*

This task (which we practised with a human-made thing, see p.55) may strike you as artificial at first. John Ruskin in the 19th century, so wary of projecting human feeling onto nature, coined a phrase for it – the 'Pathetic Fallacy' – an untruth in the realm of feeling. The French poet, Gerard de Nerval, on the other hand insisted that 'Everything is sentient. Everything has power over your being' (see p.224), – though like so many of my heroes he was just slightly crazy. If you are hesitant at first, keep grounding your words in the observational detail. Don't just write about the plant (we have already done that); don't just write about yourself. Let words arise now out of an attention to what happens in the air between you. How do you breathe when facing it? Note the differences between it and you; the similarities. Recall the work we did with elemental gestures, gravity and levity, flowing or forming qualities, mood of colour – all this can be a language now. And the aim is – to meet the plant more closely (not just any plant, but this particular one) and, like wrestlers do, to know yourself more truly through the encounter. The task does indeed require that 'willing suspension of disbelief' that Coleridge spoke about (see p.90), but the quality of these examples banish any doubts I have regarding the reality and value of such a correspondence:

**Dear Clematis,**

Today I see that you have changed. Your rounded, pink edges are gathering as if you draw them back into yourself. I have admired your beauty, but today for the first time I want to move closer to you, to bridge this distance between us, to touch your fraying. I close my eyes for a moment to imagine your perfection of yesterday, but I cannot. You are as I see you today. I move closer and breathe you for the first time... a faint wash of honey sweetness, transparent, ethereal, as if you live now more fully in the air about you than in your fading form. I have spent many hours these past days, here with you, observing, telling myself things about you... words surrounding words... surrounding you with me. You showed me my pinks and blooms, and for long moments I relived my shadows in yours. But never in all those moments did I really see you. Never did I ask, 'Is it alright that I sit here?' 'Am I blocking the sun from reaching you?' 'Have you anything to say?' Though these words you will never hear, can you feel my admiration... and my apology? Flower, are you looking at me? I think today we will meet, on this the final hour of my gazing. I think you have seen me, waiting here to lose myself and know you. My straggled thoughts have run their course and we meet here, now, I as present as you have always been. I have named you, flower. I have seen and described. There was safety in the naming. I stood, strong in myself, and named you with my words. Now the words have stopped. The names are as if in a foreign tongue. I am lost in this silence. I am growing smaller, flower, smaller than you, small enough to climb inside your cross of petals... to meet my insignificance. Here, in this dark, warm place, I can barely see, but I can feel. I feel myself being drawn into you... through you... with you... into the stream of hot life you burn through the brittle vine you grow upon... together we stream into the Earth. I feel your ancient-ness. I feel my own. I feel the love, and joy, and crushing pain of knowing all this bloom will go, but you and I will remain, transformed but never ending. This... this is what you have come to tell me, to tell all of us. I know where you go when the blossom fades. I draw back from you now, flower, and can see our forms again. Upon the vine you are but a single star in a daytime constellation, but there is a knowingness between us. For a moment, Christ-flower, you stretched wide and bade me enter unclothed through your portal and there, in utter nothingness, you spoke to me in a clear voice. And now, though you are drifting away, I see that your bloom was just an eye opening on the world for a moment and that your journey, our journey, goes on. I will watch, flower, till you are gone. I know that one day, when I take the time to really see, I will find myself naked before you again. I will grow very small, climb inside, and perhaps find my soul's hieroglyph inscribed there... and I will lose my separateness... and I will remember.

*Claudine Whiting*

Don't be surprised, though, if the sense of alienation actually grows as you do this. All sorts of projections and emotions can rise to the surface – anger that the flower is so beautiful when the world is not; or that your own human frailties stand out more starkly in the presence of that purity. No need to dismiss such feelings as unworthy. Write them down, and once again observe which feelings tell you about yourself and which about the world:

**Hello Buttercup,**

Well, how else would I greet you? Would you rather be called just Flower? At least 'Buttercup' has some recognition, some assurance that it is you I see. Although, you know, I keep looking towards the nettles. Those beings with edgy leaves. They do appeal to me, with poison and all. I know how to draw their healing forces, but that process demands my presence. I have stung my lips on a spoonful. What about you? Well, you were close to the nettles, and they had no visible flower. You were hard to miss, one yellow call among green. When I saw you I felt decided for, and I turned my back on you thinking – 'Oh no you don't!' But of course I knew I was kidding myself. I seem destined to gather the lonely ones, the left-over-and-outs. I also need to dine in abundance you know, and not always feed only on scraps and pieces. Can't you see the outline of bone in my skin? And so, I'm showing you a hard surface, mocking you for being just one on your own. Not bearing to be with you and yet not bearing to leave. If you could speak, what would it be? Do you prefer to be seen through anger, or not at all? Do you think the patience you are bound to live with will finally work through my surface? Beware, I'm telling you. Be careful. Look before planting your roots. Patches of quicksand lurk beneath harshness and seemingly solid ground.

*Marte Tveter*

X 52.   **I mentioned wrestling. We can do it here, with wooden rods stretched between our hands and those of a partner.**
Call it conversation, if you like – between I and You – moving in response to each other. It's easy just to dance or flap our arms around, and that can be enjoyable; but to enliven the space between (as we attempted in the letter to the plant) requires our willed and yet still playful inter-est, the ability to 'be between'. Wrestling with your eyes shut (either one or both of you) can help in this. As with the blindfold walking and the blindfold drawing, it allows the awakening of a more listening, peripheral consciousness.

## A posy of poesy

You don't have to look far in English poetry to find a language twined about with flowers. We have already worked with Wordsworth's famous 'Daffodils' poem (see p.53). You can find it also in Keats's 'Ode to a Nightingale', (see p.159) where he allows himself a whole verse to indulge in the names of the invisible arboretum beneath his feet.

X 53.   **Make a poem in which the plant you have chosen is named in every verse:**

**Two Ways of Looking at a Buttercup**

1.  Touching my palm with gold,
    my senses with slenderness,
    the buttercup sleeps in my waking.


2.  Taller than I was, the buttercups
    nodded their crowns
    in my grandmother's garden.

*PM with Marte Tveter*


**Five Ways of Looking at the Columbine**

1.  Gloomy purple face – it is the columbine,
    standing there all day
    thinking that night has come already.


2.  The night is changing with the blue stars.
    The saddest wind comes to the columbine.
    Tears gleam on his face.


3.  The bright-eyed columbine
    is singing under the endless sky.
    Even the moon can hear him.


4.  Gentle purple flower!
    Don't pretend not to be.
    The whole world
    knows your name.


5.  Sweet and slow was the time
    between us, columbine.
    Patient and expectant were our nights.
    A smile came from heaven.

*Yun Hee Kim*

The form here is inspired by the famous, and much imitated, poem, 'Thirteen Ways of Looking at a Blackbird',[6] by Wallace Stevens.

It still comes to me as a question, though, whether a poetry of flowers is relevant in our technological age. When I confessed this to a friend, he said, 'You make it relevant.' Here, then, as modern man in a Bluebell wood, is my attempt to do so:

**Finding out a Joy**
As I walked out this May morning
I heard the Blackbird
calling from the wood

and there without a word
the Bluebells spread and I said
look at me you pure inquisitors

and this they did –
their mute gaze finding out a joy
I'd too long shaded from the view

and as the Blackbird
carolled in the sunlit glade
I wept for being seen through.

*PM*

It starts in archaic mode, for sure, but the line about the 'pure inquisitors' just about saves it, I reckon. It is the one line I really had to work and wait for. The whole poem arises out of the imaginative practice, recommended before (see p.96), of letting the world look at us, rather than putting things in their place with our busy eyesight.

## For there is a language of flowers

Here, from *Hamlet*, is what Ophelia, well-versed in the language of flowers, speaks in her madness:

> There's Rosemary, that's for remembrance. Pray you, love, remember. And there's pansies, that's for thoughts... There's fennel for you, and columbines. There's rue for you, and here's some for me. We may call it herb of grace o' Sundays. O, you must wear your rue with a difference. There's a daisy. I would give you violets, but they withered all when my father died.[7]

The Victorians delighted in making long lists of flowers, explaining the nuances of human feeling that each one stands for. That is the intellect at work, seeking to impose its measures upon a language which, like dream, is reluctant to stand still. If, however, we take up Rudolf Steiner's recommendation of regarding natural objects as aspects of the earth's physiognomy, we might come to a more lively understanding. Just as a smile on a human face is the outer expression of an inward happiness, so we can contemplate what inwardness of the earth is winking, frowning, laughing at us, loving us through rose or daisy. Just for a moment Botticelli's Venus, so engaged with her springtime work, turns and looks at us out of the picture (see p.26).

X 54.   **Use water-colours or pastels to create a picture of your plant in flower, exaggerating its expression.** If, as Gerard de Nerval says (see p.224), 'Each flower is a soul in nature bloomed forth', then you could imagine what would happen if the colours and gestures of that soul were no longer rooted to the ground, but allowed to expand and range freely. Or what if you painted the scent of it?

Thou perceivest the Flowers put forth their precious Odours,
And none can tell how from so small a center come such sweets,
Forgetting that within that Center Eternity expands
Its ever during doors...[8]

*William Blake*

## 'The vegetable glass of nature'[9]

At this point in our plant project we drove to nearby Wakehurst Place (country cousin of the famous Kew Gardens in London) to see the flowering world in its springtime glory. There were some signs on the driveway there which said 'look both ways' and, as I happen to rather enjoy looking at signs 'both ways', I decided the meaning of this one was that, besides studying all the Latin names pinned to the tree trunks, we should find flowering shrubs in the garden that mirrored the being of each person in our group. We found a blue bush for Louise, and she said thank you because she was very grateful that we had seen into her heart so deeply. Another of our company just happened to be called 'Mi', so we took a photograph of her beside a yew tree, and called it 'Yew and Mi'. It was not just the trees which had names stuck onto them –

Wakehurst Place

there were plenty of benches, each one dedicated to the memory of a dead person who once loved this garden. I thought of my friend George, who, though still alive, has (in another garden) dedicated a bench in his own name, and goes there to remember himself.

In the teashop afterwards I asked Kira what she preferred, nature or cake, and she said nature. She also liked nature better than art, because nature came first. I tried to persuade her otherwise, saying that sunflowers did not know how to do it properly until Van Gogh painted them, but she would have none of it.

That was a good day we had together, but for fear of being too precious let me juxtapose it with the desperation that can arise when names do not so easily fall into their places:

Neglecting now to sound their lovely syllables,
we have turned Elm to lament, Ash, Oak
into a broken syntax.

We have soured the Saxon's ground.

Their syllable could stand closer up to a thing,
probing through the knotted grain
to where the un-thing stood.

Crashing among the boughs folk heard
Woden himself, giddy with rune-making.

That was long ago. We with our sour rain
have stripped rune from leaf, leaving it bereft
of what could best sustain it.

Elm. Ash. Oak. For love of these I'm overwhelmed,
ashamed to leave their names unspoken.[10]

*PM*

# *Kindling our lingo*

Christopher Smart, you will remember, said 'the right names of flowers are yet in heaven. God make gardners better nomenclators' (see p.112). The truth of this had become apparent to us through our adventure among the Latin appellations of the day before. The intention to clarify through classification is not to be dismissed, of course - it is the first 'Earth' mode of observation that we ourselves have exercised in more simple form (see p.61), and our useful modern dictionaries arise out of the practice of it. But let me introduce you now to a more fiery lexicon:

## The true names of flowers

In the ancient Norse 'Edda' there is a wisdom contest between the God, Thor, and Alvis, wisest of the dwarves. Thor keeps saying, yes, we know what humans call things... 'moon, wind, sleep... ' but what do the Gods call them? It seems important to know what giants, elves and dwarves (the 'Un-Things') call them. Alvis (All Wise) answers in the riddling form known as a 'kenning':

> What is fire called, so fierce to men,
> In all the worlds there are?

> Fire by men, Flame by gods,
> The Flickering One by vanes,
> The Wolfish by giants, All-Burner by elves,
> In Hel, the Corpse-Destroyer.[11]

Clearly, the creative, elemental beings prefer verb and metaphor to the nouny fixities that we humans use, coming closer thereby to the 'right names yet in heaven' that Smart was listening for. Delvers into etymology will know that many traces of such elvish activity are to be found lurking beneath the skin of seemingly abstract epithets – *daisy* ('Day's Eye') being a good example.

X 55.  **Try this now in relation to the plant that you have chosen. You can call upon those same beings to do the naming, or you could introduce children, madmen, teachers, psychiatrists etc. – it would be good to know how they perceive the world:**

> What is the Rose called, that we see
> In all the Worlds there are?

> Rose by Men, Flowering Heart by Gods,
> Giants call it Poignant Beauty,
> Five Ways by Dwarves, Earth-Blush by elves,
> Thorn-Fire it is called in Hel.

Yes, don't forget to search out the underworld slang for it (the letter to the buttercup, see p.117, is an example of how flowers can torment as well as bless).

X 56.  **Draw your plant with your eyes shut,** first moving your hand over the page without touching. When you have found the flow and balance of it you can let your crayon leave its traces. They are likely to be more verb-like than the first drawings that we attempted (see p.107). In that case, you could inscribe your new namings into the picture.

Hellebore: drawn with eyes shut

X 57.  To participate in something of the pointing gesture that
       the plant reveals in its topmost leaves as it prepares for
       flowering, and in its later contracting into the seed, throw
       a ball, one bounce, back and forth between you. Once the
       rhythm is established you can turn really silly and speak
       the names of flowers, trees, vegetables into the movement.

X 58.  Make a poem (or short paragraph) in which the 'I' of
       your plant becomes articulate, speaking it own true name
       and nature and potential:

**Forget-me-not**

| | | |
|---|---|---|
| Forget me | | Look beyond the blue |
| not is | | into my yellow star |
| what I | * | and then to the black |
| both am | | eye at my centre where |
| and say. | | you and I both are. |

If this is done devotedly you might well find that your speaking for the plant will begin to speak for you, interpreting aspects of your being that you did not know. In this last looking into the 'vegetable glass of nature'[12] the fairest of them all might turn out, after all, to be yourself:

No one knows my name

My name is secret

hidden inside the wind that blows through me

My leaves protect my roots, so that I won't blow away

but I want to fly with the wind

like the small insects, free and wild

Maybe then someone would know my name

but still I stand here

My head high lifted, covered in stars

this is my destiny

born to be beautiful

but inside this beauty, I long

to hear my name.

*Silje Austroll*

One night during this project a member of the group dreamed that behind her flower there was another flower. My reading of this is that she herself was the flower revealed behind it.

X 59.  Now incorporate your poem into a drawing or painting of your plant. A model for this can be found in William Blake's illustrated *Songs of Innocence and of Experience*,[13] or in the way that word and image are so combined so beautifully in the art of eastern cultures.

Hellebore

Christmas Rose, heart lifter
In time of cold and snow
Your star brings hope and glow

Lenten Rose, you take me through
The darkest times, through death,
Promising an Easter breath.

**Hellebore** (vii)

*Margaret Shillan*

## Realising potential

There is a danger of becoming so enamoured of the flowering stage of the plant that we fail to follow the process further. The colour and scent of the petals, momentary though they are, seem to promise eternal beauty and fulfilment, and yet (according to the tempter, Mephistopheles, in Goethe's *Faust*[14]) as soon as we say, 'Oh, moment stay! Thou art so beautiful!' our souls are in jeopardy. The best poets, I think, do move on beyond the sentimentality and nostalgia that too long a lingering in the Airy mode of perception might tempt us into. Christopher Smart, for instance, when he says, 'For flowers are medicinal' (see p.112), points us beyond 'glory in the flower' towards an encounter with the plant's healing or harming potential. Our attempts to intuit the essential name and nature of a plant certainly touch the fringes of what we have characterised as the Fire mode, but there is something more, a deeper level of responsibility:

> **Hellebore (viii):** Helleborus Niger; also called Setter-Wort, Setter Grass, Bear's Foot, Christmas Herb and Christmas Flower. Herb of Saturn, and 'therefore no marvel if it has some sullen conditions with it, and would be far safer being purified by the alchemist than given raw.' Goat's milk an antidote if too much taken. Roots effective against agues and madness, falling sickness, leprosy, gout, sciatica and convulsions. Roots beaten to powder and strewed upon foul ulcers, it eats away the dead flesh and instantly heals them, nay, it helps gangrene in the beginning.[15]
>
> *Nicholas Culpeper*

> **Hellebore (ix):** The day I walked out to choose my plant I scratched an itch on my arm and, though I was unaware of it, this made it bleed. I was walking with a group of people, many of whom I did not know, and then I discovered I had blood on

my hand. I checked my nose. I checked my fingers and thumbs. Had I cut myself picking through things to find my plant? I had not. I felt ashamed to think I was bleeding, and confused I did not know where or why. Only later did I connect the name of the plant that I had chosen – 'Christmas Rose' – to the inherited blood condition that I sometimes suffer from which is named the 'Christmas factor'. Rudolf Steiner said if you have an illness due to some imbalance in an organ system, go out into nature and find a plant which has a similar imbalance, squeeze the juice and it will bring you healing. Had I intuited something of this? Can it be that simple?

*Richard Heys*

Direct perception at this level would entail, no doubt, years of deep contemplation, or a long commitment to a training in biodynamic farming, Goethean observation, or herbal medicine. It is beyond the scope of this book to delve further here, but it is my hope that the artistic sense we have been schooling can be of service to anyone working with those sciences.

## Fruiting

Just as the plant at the end of its process gathers its fiery forces into fruit and seed, so, coming to the end of these two weeks of work, we devoted a morning to the presentation of our individual plant projects. Although many of our springtime pictures were by now hanging beside Botticelli's on the wall, we decided to make a tour of the garden and share the fruits of our work in the presence of the plant we had chosen. I have often found that at such times, vulnerable though they are, individuals find the courage to stand within their own authentic fire and speak it.

## The life of things

I wonder if you have ever experienced moments when space seems to turn inside out and, instead of being a small speck of dust in an endless empty universe, you feel that the here and now in which you are standing becomes the heart of everything. I say this because, standing in a corner of the wood below the Ha-Ha, bending our ears towards the one presenting her project, we had the distinct impression that the nettles, too, and the surrounding trees, were also leaning closer. Easy to laugh this away, but in a place named *Ha-Ha* anything might happen. In that interlude between field and garden, silly becomes serious, and we get a sense of what Wordsworth meant by saying that sometimes he saw, beyond physical surfaces, 'into the life of things'.[16]

The Ha-Ha

This universe in small – we have already encountered it in Milne's description of Galleon's Lap (see p.10), and in Jonson's experience at Penshurst Place. Here is Victor Hugo's version of it:

> I forgot for a long time the vast landscape spread out before me, in my preoccupation with a plot of grass on which I was seated, atop a wild little knoll of a hill. Here, too, was an entire world. Beetles were advancing slowly under deep fibres of vegetation; pear-shaped hemlock flowers imitated the pines of Italy... a poor, wet bumble-bee in black and yellow velvet, was laboriously climbing up a thorny branch, while thick clouds of gnats kept the daylight from him; a bluebell trembled in the wind and an entire nation of aphids had taken shelter under an enormous tent... I watched an earthworm that resembled an antediluvian python, come out of the mud and writhe heavenward, breathing in the air. Who knows, perhaps it, too, in its microscopic universe, has its Hercules to kill... In short, this universe is as large as the other one.[17]

# Notes

[1] Steiner, R., *How to Know Higher Worlds*, Anthroposophic Press, 1994, p.40

[2] Keats, J., *Letters of John Keats*, Oxford University Press, 1979, p.36

[3] Smart, C., *Jubilate Agno*, Rupert Hart-Davis, 1954, p.105

[4] Boswell, J., *The Life of Samuel Johnson*, Everyman's Library, 1993

[5] Steiner, R., *Michaelmas and the Soul Forces of Man*, Anthroposophic Press, 1982

[6] Stevens, W., *Collected Poems*, Faber and Faber, 1971, p.92

[7] Shakespeare, W., *Hamlet*, Act IV, Scene V, Signet Classics, 1963, p.138

[8] Blake, W., *Complete Writings*, Oxford University Press, 1972, p.520

[9] Ibid.

[10] Matthews, P., *The Ground that Love Seeks*, Five Seasons Press, 1996

11  Taylor, P.B., and Auden, W.H., (trans.) *The Elder Edda*, Faber and Faber, 1973, p.80

12  Blake, W., *Complete Writings*, Oxford University Press, 1972

13  Blake, W., *Songs of Innocence and Experience*, Oxford University Press, 1970

14  von Goethe, J. W., *Faust, part 1*: 'verweile doch, du bist so schon'.

15  Culpeper, N., *Culpeper's Complete Modern Herbal*, W. Foulsham and Co. Ltd., p.181

16  Wordsworth, W., *The Oxford Anthology of English Literature, vol. 11*, p.146

17  Hugo, V., source not traced

# The Animals in Nature

If all the beasts were gone, man would die from a great loneliness of spirit.[1]

*Chief Seattle*

*We begin to engage with the animal kingdom, starting once again in observational mode and with remembered encounters. It soon becomes clear that the shift from plant to animal naturally animates the story-maker in us. Animals like to play, especially when young, and this gives us permission to be playful with our words in response to them, characterising what is essential rather than coldly defining them. In general the writing exercises suggested here start with the I/It mode referred to earlier, and then invite us to be open to the possibility of meeting I to You.*

More than six hundred years ago John of Gaunt, Duke of Lancaster, maintained a hunting lodge on the other side of the river Medway in what was then called Lancaster Great Park. The wolves and wild boar that roamed the forest in those days are long gone, but the fallow deer that he hunted can still be met of an evening, stepping shyly out onto the fringes of the Royal Ashdown Forest Golf Course that provides the sport for today's leisured classes. Closer to home, the fox slinks along the edges of Gill's Wood, downwind of the chickens; badgers roll about in the barley (just for fun, it seems), and the long-suffering farmer is forbidden by law to do anything about it. As for birds, they are here in abundance – larks over Pixton Hill, rooks arguing in their leafy parliaments. Every August the wild geese pass back and forth along the valley between the nearby Weirwood Reservoir and Bewl Water in Kent, signing their great V's over Emerson College.

Those are the wild things. Next door, on Tablehurst Farm, we have a fine herd of brown Sussex cows that have not been deprived of their horns. Our local biodynamic farmers never tire of telling that horns are essential to the cow's work of drawing cosmic forces down into earthly matter. This is the beef herd, together with pigs, and a few sheep. Ducks and chickens waddle and cluck under the apple trees. On the far side of the village (on the other side of the Greenwich meridian, in fact) is Old Plaw Hatch Farm with its dairy herd and daily milk round. Just today a message dropped through my letterbox explaining that milk from a cow with horns does not cause allergies. I asked a former colleague, Pat Thomson, to explain in a few words what such a farm is:

> A biodynamic farm is, to a high degree, self-sustaining. The soil receives fertility from the animal manure to grow crops for people and livestock to eat. Special compost and field preparations are used to increase the health of soil and crops. The appropriate type and number of livestock bring different characteristics to this 'individuality', with the cow at the heart of the farm. Care is taken to encourage and nurture wildlife, flora, fauna, hedges, woodland, water and the wider environment. Even the influence of the planets and starry heavens is used to advantage. To the people who work on a biodynamic farm it is a lifelong task to get to know this individuality. They aim to be stewards of this unique place on earth and, like lovers, want to become familiar with all its nuances and characteristics and help it to fully express its being and potential.

# *A walk on the farm*

To begin our week together we walked down to Tablehurst Farm, open to whatever animal presences came towards us:

We went out this Monday morning early under blue sky, and clouds that refused to shape themselves into animals except one that was almost fish, and at first not a beast was anywhere in sight but we could hear them, birds ringing in the woods, the chiff-chaff back again, the chickens in the distance, and soon we reached the pond at the bottom of the bluebell wood and watched the surface for signs of animal disturbance. Plenty of flies there were, but no fish hungry enough to break the reflection of the birch trees. So we left that place and half way up the slope on the other side we stopped where two ducks were sleeping, their rounded bills so unlike the jab-a-jabbing beaks of the hens, and then Maria who is learning to be a farmer came down the path and we wouldn't let her pass until she told us a wise thing, so she revealed that the egg-laying chicken has personality while the edible bird has none and that was enough to permit her on her way, and when next we turned we saw two horses standing in a field on the tips of their fingernails, and around the next corner were the pigs, nude naked enough to make one young lady blush a little. Pigs are psychic Pauline said and know what's awaiting them. They didn't seem to mind it though but kept on rooting in the mud for present morsels or snoozed in hollows the same colour as themselves with 14 teats, unlike the jersey cow who has four and such pretty eyelashes, and after watching the brown bull nudge nose to nose with a sheep we turned our way homewards. At the top of the hill we met Sandra. We prodded her to see what kind of a beast she was and if she would squeak but she talked and told us that it was her task three days long to paint nothing but sheep. Funny, then, that her canvas was totally empty but the sky instead was suddenly full of them and the pond as we passed it this time had a moorhen swimming in the shadows, but we were too intent on coffee to stop and ponder it.

*PM*

X 60.  **Try a piece of free writing, drawing upon your impressions from such a walk (the piece above is an example).** If you live in a city and don't have a farm to walk in I believe an 'animal walk' would still be possible.

## *Stone, plant and beast*

We looked again at our stone and our plant, and then as I introduced the animal (in the form of a bronze dog that had been watching us for days from the top of the piano), we asked what the animal presence added to our tableau: independent movement; inner feelings that are expressed in sounds; warm blood in the mammal, not reliant on sun to maintain its warmth. Something wakes up in the animal. It looks at you. It can form a more personal relationship. In linking once more to my favourite theme of the relationship between the world and language, I ventured the notion that if stones are the nouns of the world, if flowers the adjectives, then animals must be the verbs. That is why story and drama properly begin with the animal.

## Animal anecdotes

X 61.  **Tell animal anecdotes from your lives. After doing this orally, you will find it relatively simple to animate your pens:**

> Once, as a child, playing in the garden I fell over and grazed my shin. While I was sitting on the concrete path, tearful, and nursing my wound, a green fly landed in the middle of the cut. It delicately walked over my burning skin. As I watched I wondered why it had landed precisely there. I hardly dared move, just sat and watched that tiny green creature as it explored the grazed and scratched surface of my right shin. Eventually I felt brave enough to try and shoo it away. I began by blowing at it. It scarcely moved at first, so I tried to whoosh it away with my hand. Suddenly that green fly took off into the air. I picked myself up and went into the house where my mother washed and dressed my wound. I never saw that green fly again.
>
> *Pauline Roach*

(For a metamorphosis of this piece, see p.210.)

Upon reflection afterwards, we were stuck by the amount of sadness, disgust, fear, surprise, tenderness, all sorts of powerful emotions, that rose up in us as we listened.

## *Bird song*

A view of Pixton Hill

The building that houses our Agriculture Course has been named 'Carson' in honour of Rachel Carson who, in her book, *Silent Spring*,[2] heroically drew attention to the harmful effects of agricultural fertilisers and pesticides. Here on Pixton Hill, I am glad to say, the spring is far from silent – thrushes and blackbirds filling the air with their songs, and not just filling it, but (it is my impression) building spatial architecture with their song-lines, making habitable what would otherwise be without bounds and soulless, and we respond accordingly:

11 o'clock. And the birds
have a song to sing
that never mentions suffering

as though this world, so
lush and alive, were enough
to quench love-longing.

*with Selkie O'Mira*

Songs about larks or cuckoos are definitely appropriate to the season, but as I was beginning to introduce one it became clear that although some of our non-native speakers were familiar with cuckoo clocks, and sometimes felt a little cuckoo in the head, they had never in their lives encountered the living creature.

April, come he will
May, he sings all day
June, he changes his tune
July, away he'll fly.[3]

– even Simon and Garfunkel adapting this old rhyme don't seem to know that the cuckoo bird inspired it.[4]

To hear the cuckoo's 'twofold shout' over the bluebells is a quintessentially English experience and not to be missed, especially by writers intent upon opening their senses to the language that nature is. We spent some time, therefore, imagining the cuckoo together, gathering what we knew about it – that it is rarely seen, that it lays eggs in other people's nests, etc. – and sharing our experiences.

My most striking meeting with one (or maybe there *is* only one) was on May Day, years ago, when my daughters were young. We had set up a make-shift Maypole in the garden and were just taking hold of our ribbons, when a cuckoo flew out of the wood and 'cuckoo' it said, right over our heads, and with that blessing upon us we started dancing. It is not for nothing that birds, with their strong peripheral awareness, are said to fly into the future and then come back, all a-twitter with the report of it.

Maypole dancing

Here is the song we sang:

> Sumer is icumen in, / Lhude sing cuccu.
>
> Groweth sed and bloweth med and / springthe the wode nu.
>
> Sing cuccu! / Awe bleteth after lomb, lhouth
>
> After calve cu. / Bulluc sterteth, bucke verteth,
>
> Murie sing cuccu! / Cuccu, cuccu,
>
> Wel singes thu cuccu. Ne / swik thu naver nu![5]

Birds in space is a theme that we will keep coming back to.

# *The nature of animals*

As a basis for the work of these two 'Weeks' you will need to chose one animal (locally observable) for ongoing research, and spend some time actually observing it. You can gather facts and fictions about it from whatever books are available.

**X 62.  Write a descriptive and informative piece on the animal that you have chosen.**

E. Grant Watson in his book, *Animals in Splendour*, for example, gives a lively description of the Wild Pig:

> In the Old Forest, before trees were felled or houses built with gardens and parks where fine folks might walk, fir, oak, beech and holly grew thick and close, and through the underbrush, beneath the branches, herds of wild pig would grunt and rummage in moist earth and dead leaves, champing their jaws, up-thrusting dark soil. Great boars with curling tusks led the herds. Sows followed with their young, grunting and squealing, and rubbing themselves against trees trunks.[6]

Turning, then, to the eating habits of the domesticated version, he observes:

> The pig, like man, is an omnivorous feeder, as his teeth indicate. He will eat a rat, if he can catch it… He is a bit of a scavenger, and will relish, as a fox will, the afterbirth of a cow. He loves apples and any kind of fruit, and, although when confined in a sty he is fed on monotonous meal-mixtures, he will relish a lump of coal, if some considerate pig lover will provide.[7]

A pig lover he is, not just the cold observer. There is, however, a danger that modern demands for scientific objectivity can blind us to the actual living creature and stultify the language that we use. Charles Dickens in his book, *Hard Times*, famously caricatures this through the mouth of Bitzer, a boy who (trained too soon in adult methods) defines a horse into the bits that his name prepares us for:

> Quadruped. Graminivorous. Forty teeth, namely twenty-four grinders, four eye-teeth and twelve incisive. Sheds coat in the spring; in marshy countries sheds hoofs too. Hoofs hard, but requiring to be shod with iron. Age known by marks in mouth.[8]

The facts are enumerated accurately enough, but the agility of the tongue employed to do so is no match for the speed and sleekness of the beast itself. At its worst this analytical coolness towards Creation led Sir Francis Bacon, the father of modern science, to say (supposedly) that in order to discover the secrets of nature we would be justified in torturing her on the rack.[9] The consequence of such an attitude is depicted in Joseph Wright's powerful picture, *An Experiment with a Bird in the Air Pump*:[10]

Is it clear what is happening? A white cockatoo has been placed in a vacuum flask, and various people, each with a different response, gather round to see what will happen to it when the air is pumped out. The girls (whose pet bird it probably is) can barely bring themselves to watch what is happening. The young men, on the other hand, priding themselves on an enlightened attitude towards the world, manage to observe the scene without any annoying emotions intruding themselves into the experience. In the light of our on-going enterprise to develop a new participatory awareness the whole range of attitudes shown in the picture is extremely instructive.

We have noted before (see p.108) that children see meanings rather than things. The world they inhabit is sym-bolic (meaning 'thrown together'), and this is splendidly apparent in the following attempt by a young boy (not so well trained in the scientific method as poor Bitzer) to define a cow:

The Cow is a mammal and it is tame. It has six sides – right, left, fore, back, an upper and below. At the back it has a tail on which hangs a brush. This is to send the flies away so that they will not fall into the milk. The head is for the purpose of growing horns and so that the mouth can be somewhere. The horns are to butt with. The mouth is to moo with. Under the Cow hangs the milk. It is arranged for milking. When people milk the milk comes, and there is never an end to the supply. How the Cow does it I have not yet realised, but it makes more and more. The Cow has a fine sense of smell. You can smell it far away. This is the reason for fresh air in the country. The man Cow is called an Ox. It is not a mammal. The Cow does not eat much, but what it eats it eats twice so that it gets enough. When it is hungry it moos, and when it says nothing it is because all its inside is full up of grass.[11]

This is poetry and science in one. Out of childhood *innocence* he names each part of that cow in purposeful relationship to its environment. Very different is the dia-bolic ('thrown apart') world that we adults, fallen into the world of *experience*, spend our days walking up and down in. But look at the figure in the bottom right hand corner of Joseph Wright's painting. Is he not someone who (while not rejecting the scientific consciousness in our times) wonders how compassion and participation can be included in the experimental process?

We can let Ralph Waldo Emerson have a chance to speak here:

> But when a faithful thinker, resolute to detach every object from personal relations, shall, at the same time, kindle science with the fire of the holiest affections, then will God go forth again into Creation.[12]

## *Science and poetry*

A book that I have found especially helpful as a bridge between science and poetry is Wolfgang Schad's *Man and Mammals*.[13] We probably all carry, half consciously, a sense for the qualities of the different animals. Schad lifts this into consciousness by pointing out that the three main classes of mammals each emphasise a particular aspect of the bodily organism:

> **Rodents**, with their nibbling incisors and sensitive whiskers, are obviously creatures highly awake in their nerves and senses.
> **Carnivores**, with the pronounced development of canine teeth, and their rhythmic movement, are creatures of heart and lung.
> **Ungulates**, with their powerful molars, spend all their forces in their limbs (horses) and metabolism (cows).

These can also be sub-divided: e.g. of the ungulates the cow is the most metabolic, the horse being more nerve/sense, and the pig embodying something of the carnivore.

Schad makes no conscious attempt to be a poet, but so interesting are the facts he presents that it is impossible not to feel there must be a great love and intelligence, some ordering Logos, at work behind the tapestry of nature.

Those who wish to deepen their ability to read it would do well to seek out the work of Craig Holdredge. His *Nature Institute* has published a number of articles on particular animals, including his work on the elephant referred to earlier (see p.6). Here is a further passage from that book, showing how the whole declares itself in every part:

> There is no more physically flexible organ in the animal kingdom than the elephant's trunk. While the trunk is clearly the elephant's focal instrument for living out its flexible nature, this paramount elephantine feature in fact expresses itself in the whole animal – physically, physiologically, and behaviourally. The elephant does not eat food of one type, it can shift from one food source to another; when given the opportunity it goes for variety. The elephant can live in different habitats – from the climatically uniform and food-rich rain forest to the extremes and dearth of the desert. But most elephants live in the more rhythmically changing savannah and monsoon climates, where they move with the changing seasons and the changing sources of food the seasons bring.[14]

## Animal characters

We alluded earlier (see p.6) to the difference between definition and characterisation. The boy's piece about the cow is surely an example of the latter.

## X 63.  Characterise an animal through the difference between it and another species.

W.H. Hudson, on the domesticated pig:

> I have a friendly feeling towards pigs generally, and consider them the most intelligent of beasts... I also like his disposition and attitude towards other creatures, especially man. He is not suspicious or shrinkingly submissive, like horses, cattle and sheep; nor an impudent devil-may-care like the goat; nor hostile like the goose, or condescending like the cat; nor flatteringly parasitic like the dog. He views us from a totally different, a sort of democratic standpoint, as fellow citizens and brothers, and takes it for granted, or grunted, that we understand his language.[15]

Here is Walt Whitman lamenting the difference being animal existence and the human condition:

> I think I could turn and live awhile with the animals
> ... they are so placid and self-contained.
> I stand and look at them long and long.
>
> They do not sweat and whine over their condition,
> They do not like awake in the dark and weep for their sins,
> They do not make me sick discussing their duty to God,
> Not one is dissatisfied... not one is demented with
>     the mania of owning things,
> Not one kneels to another nor to his kind that lived thousands
>     of years ago,
> Not one is respectable or unhappy over the whole earth.[16]

A lively discussion would arise if you simply considered the difference between a dog and a cat. Winston Churchill memorably observed that 'dogs look up to you; cats look down on you; pigs treat you as equals.'

**X 64. It is also possible to characterise a creature through likenesses. The scientist does this by drawing attention to extraordinary facts:**

> The female elephant has two mammary glands that are situated between the forelegs, that is, in the same positions as in humans. This is unique among four-legged, non-arboreal mammals.[17]

Craig Holdredge

The poet does it through simile and metaphor:

**War God's Horse Song**
I am the Turquoise Woman's son.
    On top of Belted Mountain
    Beautiful horses – slim like a weasel!
    My horse with a hoof like a striped agate,
    With his fetlock like a fine eagle plume:
    My horse whose legs are quick lightning
    Whose body is an eagle-plumed arrow:
    My horse whose tail is like a trailing black cloud.
    The Little Holy Wind blows thru his hair.
    My horse with a mane made of short rainbows.
    My horse with ears made of round corn.
    My horse with eyes made of big stars.
    My horse with a head made of mixed waters.
    My horse with teeth made of white shell.
    The long rainbow is in his mouth for a bridle
        & with it I guide him.
    When my horse neighs, different-coloured horses follow.

When my horse neighs, different-coloured sheep follow.
I am wealthy because of him.

> Before me peaceful
> Behind me peaceful
> Under me peaceful
> Over me peaceful –
> Peaceful voice when he neighs.
> I am everlasting & peaceful
> I stand for my horse.[18]

*Navaho*

Lightning; holy wind; mixed waters; white shell – all powers of the elements are gathered in this horse! There is a great nobleness and reverence about the poem – another example, perhaps, of Rousseau's 'Noble Savage' speaking the 'real language of men' (see p.51 and p.195).

**X 65.  As a help in shaking off any tendency to static definition, take some of the adjectives and adverbs that appear in the piece by W.H Hudson –** *suspicious… shrinkingly… submissive… impudent… hostile… flattering…* **and move with those qualities, or simply walk like various animals and try in the group to guess which is which. Play with animal modes, with their tempos and temperaments, in the throwing of beanbags to one another.**

**X 66.  Draw with your eyes shut the animal that you have chosen.**

In these ways the verb nature that is so characteristic of the animal realm can be released into the next, somewhat playful, stage of our writing.

## *Larking about*

### X 67. Open up an animal word.

| | | | |
|---|---|---|---|
| Lambs | Lambs | Tigers | Tigers |
| Are | Astound | Immediately | Inch |
| Meek | Mountains | Gain | Gingerly |
| Beneath | By | Everyone's | Ensuring |
| Stars | Skipping | Respectful | Red |
| | | Silence | Surprise |

Now try it with the particular animal that you have chosen.

### X 68. Give five words to your writing partner and receive five words back. Words not normally associated with animals would serve best:

*Daisy/Brook/Fur/Nose/Rope* and
*Socrates/Bread/Silence/Chair/Thoughtful*

**Now write a characterisation of a particular animal in alternating phrases, sentences or lines with your partner, using (in whatever order) the words you have been given:**

**Cow**: It is well known that cows eat <u>daisies</u>, so that leaves more <u>bread</u> for me. It is also well known that cows have <u>noses</u>, and what does it mean then that <u>Socrates</u> also had a nose? Yes, he had a nose for the truth, but as for <u>fur</u>, he had very little of that. Yes, but they both have a nose for listening, each sitting in <u>silence</u> as one listens to the earth and stars and the other to thought. Unlike those Greek philosophers the cows says yes of course you can step twice into the same <u>brook</u>. It is their <u>thoughtful</u> burden that prevents those philosophers from diving

again into the same waters. I am not going to throw a <u>rope</u> to save them. The cow has all the philosophy I need, and maybe she'll teach me to put aside the <u>chair</u> I sit in that raises me from the ground, and bow my body to the earth.

*PM with Maryse Arnold*

Such a task can help us break out of habitual modes, and if it wanders into chaos we can always break the rules afterwards and rework it:

> Did Socrates eat daisies?
> A cow eats daisies
> and certainly both Socrates and the cow
> have a nose for the truth.
> A nose for listening,
> each sitting in silence,
> one hearkening to the Earth,
> the other to stars.
> Do they hear different voices?
> Philosophers say, 'Chairs don't exist',
> or, 'You cannot step twice into the same brook'.
> The cow says, 'Of course they do, of course you can'.
> These philosophers, it is their thoughtful burden
> that prevents them from diving again and again
> into those waters.

A cow has all the philosophy I need –
head bowed to the Earth, horns
tipped with starlight.

*Maryse Arnold*

## Questing

Sometimes detached statements about an event no longer suffice, and we feel the need to address a creature directly. Here are some words which came to me one night after investigating a strange scraping noise at my sitting-room window:

**Snail**:

Is it you, little snail? – dragging your spiral house across the stars.
It makes me smile that such a lowly one should live so earnestly,
And that a sound so intimate could quite drown out the empty
        roar of night.

X 69.  **Put the name of your chosen animal at the top of a piece of paper, and pass it around the group. Write a few questions to the animal on each page as it reaches you:**

**Frog:**

Which do you prefer – hopping or swimming?
Have you ever been kissed?
Are you the world's most naked thing?
Is ugliness a form of beauty?
Would pondering ponds make us all turn green?
Who taught you to play the Ukulele?

Once you have done so you can edit and augment what you received. William Blake gives us the archetypal model for such a questing:

**The Tyger**

Tyger! Tyger! Burning bright
In the forest of the night,
What immortal hand of eye
Could frame thy fearful symmetry?

In what distant deeps or skies
Burnt the fire of thine eyes?
On what wings dare he aspire?
What the hand dare seize the fire?

And what shoulder, & what art,
Could twist the sinews of thy heart?
And when thy heart began to beat,
What dread hand? & what dread feet?

What the hammer? What the chain?
In what furnace was thy brain?
What the anvil? What dread grasp
Dare its deadly terrors clasp?

When the stars threw down their spears,
And water'd heaven with their tears,
Did he smile his work to see?
Did he who made the Lamb make thee?

Tyger! Tyger! Burning bright
In the forests of the night,
What immortal hand or eye,
Dare frame thy fearful symmetry?[19]

In his *Songs of Innocence* you can find a similar poem addressed to the Lamb.[20] Clearly the *difference between* Lamb and Tiger was a very present question for him.

X 70.  Blake's poem is in rhyming couplets. When W.B. Yeats was asked where he got his good ideas from he said, 'from the rhyming', so to make such a poem (possibly alternate lines with a partner) might be yet another way of looking newly at a creature.

## Praising and lamenting

We have been shifting gradually from observational work towards exclamations and expressions of feeling, and there is no need now to hold back from that. To warm this up a repetitive form could be helpful:

X 71.  Make some apologies:

**Snail**:
Forgive me for rushing past you.
I'm sorry I put my wellbeing before yours in the lettuce patch.

X 72.  Give some 'thank yous' to your chosen animal.

**Snail**:
Thank you for your nomadic teachings.
Thanks for your trail of silver.
Thank you for showing me how slow a creature can move
and for allowing me to use your empty home as a necklace.

From praise to lamentation – this is the range of feeling that, according to Rilke, is the lyric poet's task to articulate. Wishes could also be included. These repetitive forms are only a way in. Once you have warmed to the task you can do it more freely.

## Creative imperatives

On Mount Sinai Moses received Ten Commandments to help us live up to our full human potential.[21] Many of them are in the form of 'Thou shalt not', but why should they have to be? And what if other creatures besides humans were to receive such creative imperatives?

X 73.  **Give some commandments to the animal you have chosen. You could imagine some divine creative being (even if you don't believe in one) calling upon the verb nature uniquely embodied in each animal to come to expression. You can do this by passing the paper round again, or individually:**

**Snail**:
Never leave home.
Climb up your spiral staircase.
Whirl in your own way.
Think slime sublime.
Don't catch up with the rabbit.

**Caterpillar**:

Measure a leaf inch by inch
Think butterfly within your lowliness.

**Fox**:

And god said let there be fox cub
The colour of warm, dry sand,
Let him have a beard of white swansdown
And in his mouth the knowledge of milk-trust.
Let his nose go into the truth of things,
May it find me in the nest of a green meadow
Under golden tongues of dandelion in full flowering,
The sweet and the stink of them.

May he be satisfied with fowl flesh
Warm in his mouth, the living blood of it
A taste of my substance alive and running in him.
May he grow in cunning,
Keen as the hunger in his belly.
It is my hunger.
May he be satisfied with good things.

Let him run like an arrow from the red hunter
And when the hour comes, if it must come,
That he is torn from himself,
His heart thrown to the dogs,
Let him hear close by, and closer still,
The sound of his name sung from the breast,
And the last word be mine: beloved.

*Andie Lewenstein*

# The penetralium of mystery

The poetic act of talking to the animals takes classic form in the 'Ode to a Nightingale', by John Keats. Written in mid-May (the very season that we are in) it is an archetypal expression of how it feels to move, in imagination, through the outer threshold of nature, as opposed to the inner one that Coleridge crossed in his 'Kubla Khan experience' (see p.90). In carrying the earthly image of the nightingale through what he calls elsewhere the 'penetralium of mystery',[22] Keats comes into an ecstasy, and in doing so almost dies to himself, becomes nothing (the whole poem is full of funereal imagery). When he does eventually come back to himself he feels all the more solitary. Coleridge in writing his great poem was, so he claims, awake in his sleep. Keats on the other hand, when writing his ode (if I read the ending rightly), was asleep within his waking. This state will be familiar to those who meditate. Here it makes its appearance, perhaps as poetic grace, possibly as intentional poetic practice. We will encounter it again when we consider the relationship between fairy tale and everyday life (see p.219):

### Ode: To a Nightingale

My heart aches, and a drowsy numbness pains
My sense, as though of hemlock I had drunk,
Or emptied some dull opiate to the drains
One minute past, and Lethe-wards had sunk:
'Tis not through envy of thy happy lot,
But being too happy in thine happiness,
That thou, light-wingèd Dryad of the trees,
In some melodious plot
Of beechen green, and shadows numberless,
Singest of summer in full-throated ease.

O for a draught of vintage! that hath been
Cool'd a long age in the deep-delvèd earth,
Tasting of Flora and the country-green,
Dance, and Provençal song, and sunburnt mirth!
O for a beaker full of the warm South!
Full of the true, the blushful Hippocrene,
With beaded bubbles winking at the brim,
And purple-stainèd mouth;
That I might drink, and leave the world unseen,
And with thee fade away into the forest dim:

Fade far away, dissolve, and quite forget
What thou among the leaves hast never known,
The weariness, the fever, and the fret
Here, where men sit and hear each other groan;
Where palsy shakes a few, sad, last grey hairs,
Where youth grows pale, and spectre-thin, and dies;
Where but to think is to be full of sorrow
And leaden-eyed despairs;
Where beauty cannot keep her lustrous eyes,
Or new Love pine at them beyond to-morrow.

Away! away! for I will fly to thee,
Not charioted by Bacchus and his pards,
But on the viewless wings of Poesy,
Though the dull brain perplexes and retards:
Already with thee! tender is the night,
And haply the Queen-Moon is on her throne,
Cluster'd around by all her starry Fays
But here there is no light,
Save what from heaven is with the breezes blown
Through verdurous glooms and winding mossy ways.

I cannot see what flowers are at my feet,
Nor what soft incense hangs upon the boughs,
But, in embalmèd darkness, guess each sweet
Wherewith the seasonable month endows
The grass, the thicket, and the fruit-tree wild;
White hawthorn, and the pastoral eglantine;
Fast-fading violets cover'd up in leaves;
And mid-May's eldest child,
The coming musk-rose, full of dewy wine,
The murmurous haunt of flies on summer eves.

Darkling I listen; and, for many a time
I have been half in love with easeful Death,
Call'd him soft names in many a musèd rhyme,
To take into the air my quiet breath;
Now more than ever seems it rich to die,
To cease upon the midnight with no pain,
While thou art pouring forth thy soul abroad
In such an ecstasy!
Still wouldst thou sing, and I have ears in vain—
To thy high requiem become a sod.

Thou wast not born for death, immortal Bird!
No hungry generations tread thee down;
The voice I hear this passing night was heard
In ancient days by emperor and clown:
Perhaps the self-same song that found a path
Through the sad heart of Ruth, when, sick for home,
She stood in tears amid the alien corn;
The same that ofttimes hath
Charm'd magic casements, opening on the foam
Of perilous seas, in faery lands forlorn.

Forlorn! the very word is like a bell
To toll me back from thee to my sole self!
Adieu! the fancy cannot cheat so well
As she is famed to do, deceiving elf.
Adieu! adieu! thy plaintive anthem fades
Past the near meadows, over the still stream,
Up the hill-side; and now 'tis buried deep
In the next valley-glades:
Was it a vision, or a waking dream?
Fled is that music: – do I wake or sleep?[23]

*John Keats*

# Notes

[1] Reputedly from a treaty oration by Chief Seattle of the Suquamish tribe

[2] Carson, R., *Silent Spring*, Penguin Books, 1966

[3] Trad., 'April, come he will'

[4] 'April, come she will' song by P. Simon, 1965

[5] Anon., 'Summer is icumen in', medieval

[6] Grant Watson, E.L., *Animals in Splendour*, John Baker, 1967, p.43

[7] Ibid.

[8] Dickens, C., *Hard Times*, Collins, 1961, p.18

[9] Bacon, F., this view is often attributed to him, but the tracing of it in his writings has proved elusive

[10] Wright, J., *An Experiment on a Bird in the Air Pump*, in the National Gallery, London, 1768

[11] Peacock, G., and Bosman, M.M., (ed.) *Modern Humour*, J.M. Dent & Sons Ltd., p.188

[12] Emerson, R.W., *Selected Prose and Poetry*, Holt, Rhinehardt and Winston, 1962, p.45

[13] Schad, W., *Man and Mammals*, Waldorf Press, 1977, p.30

[14] Holdredge, C., *The Flexible Giant*, The Nature Institute, 1977, p.30

[15] Hudson, W.H., source not traced

[16] Whitman, W., *The Complete Poems*, Penguin Books, 1983, p.94

[17]  Holdredge, C., *The Flexible Giant*, The Nature Institute, 1977, p.58

[18]  Rothenberg, J., (ed.) *Technicians of the Sacred*, Anchor Books, 1969, p.40

[19]  Blake, W., 'The Tyger' in *Complete Writings*, Oxford University Press, 1972

[20]  Ibid, p.214

[21]  *The Holy Bible*, Authorized Version, Exodus, Ch.20, verses 1-17

[22]  Keats, J., *Letters of John Keats*, Oxford University Press, 1979, p.43

[23]  Keats, J., in Barnard, J., (ed.) 'Ode: To a Nightingale' in *The Complete Poems*, Penguin Books

# Giving Voice to the Animals

I know a little language of my cat...[1]

*Robert Duncan*

*The verb nature of the animals invites us to lend them our words so that they, too, may find a voice through riddle, prayer and fable. This is the third stage (I/I) of the process that we practised earlier. The work that we began with story-making is taken further into the creation of origin stories.*

Arthur Rimbaud (before he renounced such 'absurdities') said 'the poet is responsible for the animals'.[2] When I brought this to the group somebody said, yes, we act responsibly towards them by tending to our own inner animal. I remembered something that both Rainer Maria Rilke[3] and Rudolf Steiner[4] said – that things and creatures gain intensity of existence through our devoted naming of them. Steiner even goes so far as to say that if we did not potentise the animals by naming them they would eventually die out. What he means by that I am not quite sure, but it readily comes to mind when I read in the newspapers that the cuckoo, starling and skylark are not so often heard these days. One researcher (who happened to be called Mr. Raven) gave some reasonable explanations for this decline – pollution in cities, intensive farming, roofs that no longer provide space for nesting. 71% of the sparrows gone, 72% of the starlings that used to wheel in living forms around the London chimney pots. It is loss of soul

164

that I lament, not just loss of numbers. The very openness of our hearts is surely diminished if there are no larks to hearken to, or if we can't hear them sing above the noise of traffic. *Cuckoo, jug-jug, pu-we, to witta woo* are vital syllables of Creation, embodiments and signatures of the local air that have for centuries in-formed the Aires of our greatest singers, and (to echo Chief Seattle, see p.134) when the birds that sound them are gone the shape of their absence will be a hollow within our Island's story.

Despair lies that way... or can we lend them a potent voice through which to sound their essences?

## Riddles

Sometimes when I take visitors to the 'Hundred Acre Wood' I stuff a tattered copy of *Winnie the Pooh* into my coat pocket. That handbook of the poetic art is full of animals finding their voices. One passage I like to read is where Pooh comes into conversation with that most prosaic of creatures, Kanga: 'I don't know if you are interested in Poetry at all?' 'Hardly at all,' said Kanga. And then a little further on: 'Talking of poetry,' said Pooh quickly, 'have you ever noticed that tree over there...' 'I can see a bird in it from here,' said Pooh, 'or is it a fish?'[5] Even that silly riddling question is not enough to turn her head.

X 74. **The deepest art of the riddler is to lend a voice to an animal (or object) and let it characterise itself through a question:**

> My hotel is made of string.
> No guests go out once they've come in.
> I serve no drink, I serve no meat.
> My guests provide the food I eat.

*PM*

165

Then the question comes: *Who am I?* A fish? A bird? No, a spider, of course. And thus, childwise, we open a dialogue with the world, making dull things shine through power of metaphor.

## Animal prayers

X 75. Send up some prayers from the animals that you have chosen. You can do this collaboratively at first, passing some narrow pieces of paper around, each adding one line to the prayer. A variation of this is to have only the preceding line visible to the one who receives it around the circle. In this case, write the name of the animal on the bottom right hand corner of the paper so that everyone knows which animal it is:

**Whale**:

God, it's Big Blue talking;
almost as big as you, and yet
I'm simple in my ways.
I roar and thrash and praise –
so grateful, Lord, to be
made mother of these waters.

Once the paper has gone round and back to you, you can edit and select the best bits of what was received by chance:

**Mole**:

From my dark velvet world I sometimes hear you, sighing in your sky. Here, underground, I scavenge about in my heart burrowing deeply for you.

**Pig**:

I don't begrudge my nakedness. I wish, though, you had given me the scent of lavender and a purse made out of silk and pearls.

**Crow**:

I could wish you had made me human, except for this delight I take in being blown about, waving my black handkerchief in these winds of Pentecost.

And then, having learnt from the surprising qualities that arise through such collaboration, you can attempt your own. Allow something of the tempo of the animal into your words about it:

**Mouse**:

It's me, Minikin Mouse.
Can I help you, Lord?

I wonder sometimes
whether my squeak is heard
among your spiral galaxies.
If you have need, though
for a whiskered thing
to nibble the Nebulae,
ask me. I'm ready.

*PM*

**Cow**:

Please don't take offence, Oh God, if I never gaze up towards you in the sky, for my days are spent feeling the stars in your universe spinning through my body. Even when the night sky gives itself over to day I carry on feeling those stars. These constellations dancing within me are what people see when they look into my deep dark eyes. The universe digests, always transforming; the stars blink in my bloodstream and I blink at your little creations: the flies that sit on my eyelids, the lady-bugs on the grass blades. Do not take offence if my prayers are simple and earthly, for my brain is in my belly doing its dark thing slowly. I am doing my best, Lord, to be the chalice that pours your spirit back into the thirsty soil of your creation.

*Maryse Arnold*

**Horse**:

May God say me 'Nay'
That I may know He is there

Let the hoof struck spark
Sting me to awareness

May the burdens that I bear
Weigh me down to knowledge of this earth

May my flight across the plain
Bring me to the impossible hurdle

May the proud arch of my neck
Stay yoked in service to what's true

May the power of my going
Be restrained to the one still place

May these things come about
That I may say God 'Yea'.

*Ann White*

If the concept of God or prayer is difficult for you, you could do it in the form of wishes. Or you could do the task as given, risking the 'willing suspension of disbelief' that Coleridge suggests 'constitutes poetic faith' (see p.90). The opportunity to have a 'You' to address in this way can be very powerful, and is not to be missed.

The Horse Trough at Coleman's Hatch.
The words inscribed on it are from
Coleridge's 'The Ancient Mariner':

He prayeth best, who loveth best
All things both great and small;
For the dear God who loveth us,
He made and loveth all.[6]

X 76. Make a pastel drawing of your chosen animal. Not cow, but Cowness. Not cat, but the essential verve and verb of its tail and whiskers. Out of this, you might discover a gesture which expresses the essential being of your chosen animal.

## Fable

It is ancient doctrine that what we experience as the heights and depths of our human inwardness (our emotions and passions) are spread out and imaged among the animals: 'Hog in sloth, fox in stealth, wolf in greediness, dog in madness, lion in prey',[7] is how Edgar in *King Lear* sees it. Such expressions pervade our language – stubborn as a mule, snake in the grass, chicken livered, catty – you can think of others. Mostly we use them as insults, but they can also be employed as endearments.

This practice, which surely arises spontaneously in every culture, finds more conscious form in the fable. In the group we told some of the ones we knew; Aesop's *The Hare and the Tortoise*, we all knew that one. The basic imaginative act in them is to portray human failings through exaggerated animal gestures. Yes, our moral characters might well improve on hearing such stories, but as the animal often comes off worse through the comparison I am reluctant to recommend that you attempt to write one.

More appropriate, I think, to the modern child's ear is the nature story:

A goldfish lived in a pond. Gracefully he flitted among the ripples, and as he did so his own gold colour glowed in the sunlight. When night came he looked everywhere for that light, but he could not find it. Sometimes the silvery moon gave a cool light, but on many nights the pool lay in darkness. The stars shone high in the sky, and the goldfish longed for their light but alas, they were so far away he could not reach them.

One day a bird flew near, and the goldfish asked him about the stars. 'They dwell in the sky', replied the bird. 'And when I spread my wings I can fly quite near them'. 'Will you take me with you?' asked the fish. The bird would gladly have done so, but the goldfish had only fins to swim with, no wings to spread wide in the air, so the fish had to stay in the pool while the bird filled the air with his song. But the bird did feel sorry for his new friend, so up, up he flew, even closer to the stars, to tell them about the goldfish who longed for the starlight. One of the star-children wanted to help the fish, and decided to visit him. Next morning the goldfish found a wonderful creature in the pool – white star-shapes, formed into a flower, with a golden sun-heart in the middle. She floated on a green stalk amidst leaves as round as the pool itself. How happy the goldfish was to see her. 'What is your name?' he asked her. 'My name is Waterlily', she smiled. When the fish saw that smile he said, 'Now I am happy. The stars have come down to me.'

*Reworked from a story by Eva Cohn*

X 77. **Those of you who work with children may wish to attempt such a piece in which nature is one great community of life and language.**

When Rudolf Steiner recommended such stories to people studying to be teachers, he said:

> ... between the change of teeth and the ninth or tenth year you should teach in descriptive imaginative pictures, for what the children then receive from you will live on in their minds and souls as a natural development, right through their whole lives.[8]

He calls upon educators to undertake a self-education in this ability to create living images, and then adds encouragingly that a person 'who cannot endure being clumsy and doing things stupidly and imperfectly at first, will never really be able to do them perfectly in the end out of their inner self.'

## Origin stories

For all ancient cultures the snail's spiral shell, the yellow bill of the blackbird, the stripes of the tiger, were not cold facts to be observed, but significant, and in their stories they sought to trace the unique features of the creatures back to their fiery sources. In modern times Rudyard Kipling attempted something similar in his *Just So Stories*.[9] These were published in 1902, the year that he moved to 'Batemans' in nearby Burwash, on the other side of East Sussex. Some of the titles – 'How the Elephant Got its Trunk'; 'How the Leopard Got its Spots' – will be familiar to you, I am sure.

X 78. **We worked previously with the creative will of the command. Lead this now into the creation of origin** stories, exploring distinctive features of our chosen animals, and allowing them to speak. Help each other in the group to find energising titles. Write very fast, without thinking of the ending. Or try it collaboratively, and then rework it individually once the tale is flowing. However you do it, the aim is to make stories that are somehow 'true' to the animal, not arbitrarily invented:

### Why does the Crab walk sideways?

Once upon a time crabs walked forwards, and not only did they walk forwards but they walked forwards very fast, knocking everyone else out of the way. Well, this was a very big problem for everyone. Something had to be done. And so a council of all the other animals was called and it was decided that one of them must go to the tallest mountain to ask for help. The ant went to the mountain and said 'Mountain, mountain the crab is so inconsiderate. What shall we do?' The mountain listened and thought and said 'Does anything embarrass a crab? What is it that makes a crab turn shy?' 'Oh, good,' said the ant, and scurried back home. 'Well,' said the council. 'What advice do you bring?' 'We must see through to his softness. Someone must face him. Someone must say how pink your flesh is, how tender and lovely. Someone must say dear crab, my darling, how cuddly you are, so tender-hearted.' That's what they did. The fox said it, the owl said it. The mouse said it, the grouse said it. The crab felt down into his soft pinkness and remembered all that he had hidden, all that he had shielded himself from, and he felt so thankful that his tender heart began to speak – he spoke to the whole council. He blushed in public. 'Thank you, thank you' he said, then he sidled out sideways.

*PM with Triena Wing*

And here is one which arose out of the earlier observation during our walk on the farm that the nakedness of the pig can be somewhat embarrassing:

### Why must the Pig be naked?

Once upon a time there was a dark hairy pig that wanted to be human. The pig prayed every day and every night, and she thought to herself – 'I wish I could be a beautiful woman.' The pig worked hard, digging in the ground. One day, God came to the pig and said, 'I'll give you 100 bunches of garlic and you must eat just one garlic a day. You also have to stay in a dark tunnel for 100 days. If you can be patient during these 100 days you will become a human being.' When the pig received the garlic she was so happy to have the chance to be a woman at last, but she did not like the taste of that garlic and the darkness of the tunnel. The pig waited one day, ten days, sixty days. By the time 99 days had passed she had grown so curious that she came out from the dark tunnel. She saw that her body had indeed changed and that she had human skin. 'What a beautiful naked body I have,' said the pig, and she went to the pond to look at her face reflected in the water. But, Oh dear! How shocked she was to see that although her body was beautiful she still had a pig's big snout. The pig cried desperately. 'If only I had waited one more day, my wish would have come true.' This is why, like us human beings, the pig is naked, but only half as beautiful.

*Yun Hee Kim*

After we heard them in the group we discussed whether they were true or not, and in what way such stories might be true. God must be happy with his prominent role in recent pages. I wonder what he makes of this one:

### The White Crow

It was a time when all animals feared each other and men lived in the fear of God. It was dark in those days and Creation still resounded in the silence of the wind. Most wouldn't venture far from their homes… except for the crow. The crow had no home. Or. The wind was his home. He would soar in the dark sky, wearing his white silvery plumage that struck like a flash of light the whites of the eyes of the fearful creatures. And to the wind he would blow a gentle humming, a prayer into the heart of all things. One day, while flying over the gentle slope of a valley, the wind shook loose one of his white feathers. It drifted down and found the hand of a simple man, a scribe of the laws and trials. The scribe took it with surprise and placed it amongst his inks and pens. There must have been magic to this white feather because, after that, thoughts started to trouble the scribe's nights and days, thoughts that even God, the maker of all laws, never dared to entertain, thoughts that were demanding to be written down. The man grasped the white feather, took a piece of paper, gazed inward and deeply into his thoughts and started to write. But as he wrote one word and then another, he noticed that the ink that was darkening the page was darkening the feather he wrote with. And yet he couldn't stop. He wanted to see what lay beyond the laws of God; what his own thoughts had to uncover. So he wrote and wrote... until the feather was completely black. The whole sky became black then, followed by a flash of light and a crack of thunder. In the silence after, the scribe looked up and he could see the darkness fading and a new light arising he had never seen before. Tears, welling up from his heart, ran down his face and into the earth. He heard the song of birds for the first time as they flew hesitantly from their nests and a fox skipped out of its hole. Suddenly, the scribe saw the crow in the distance, above the tree line. His feathers were black now. He had taken into himself the thoughts of the scribe, thoughts that belonged to the gates of the heart of Man.

*Alex Westerlund*

# Notes

[1] Duncan, R., *Ground Work, Before the War*, New Directions, 1984, p.98

[2] Rimbaud, A., *Collected Poems*, trans. by Bernard, O., Penguin Books, 1986, p.12

[3] Rilke, R.M., *The Duino Elegies*, trans. Leishman J.B. and Spender, S., Chatto and Windus, 1977, p.85

[4] Steiner, R., *The Meaning of Life*, Rudolf Steiner Press, 2000

[5] Milne, A.A., *Winnie the Pooh*, Mammoth, 1995, p.89

[6] Coleridge, S.T., *Poetical Works*, Oxford University Press, 1973, p.186

[7] Shakespeare, W., *King Lear*, Act III, Scene IV, Signet Classics, 1963, p.114

[8] Steiner, R., *The Kingdom of Childhood*, Rudolf Steiner Press, 1974, p.69

[9] Kipling, R., *Just So Stories*, Harper Collins, 1996

# *Being Human*

*Our progress through the realms of nature brings us now to a consideration of what it means to be human. An imagination of the human being in respectful companionship with stone, plant and beast is presented. The seasonal Whitsun festival gives us the opportunity to develop our thoughts on imagination and human creativity as we explore, through written conversation and the writing of letters, how language finds its deepest destiny as a means of communion between people. We arrive at a turning point in which 'heart work' takes forward the 'work of eyes'.*

At this point in our progress we must begin to include what our inward nature has projected into the world – the paraphernalia of our human household: spoons (they have appeared already), shoes, mirrors, buses, the tools we use, the houses and cities that we build with them. It is time now to say that the sunset over the spire of Forest Row church is made more beautiful by all the pollution in the air, the jet-trails of the planes spiralling down into nearby Gatwick airport. And the glow in the northern sky? That's the collective lights of London dimming our view of the Milky Way. William Blake, who has featured so prominently in this book, was a London poet. Often he imaged that city, with its 'chartered streets',[1] with its churches darkened by industrial soot, as a kind of hell, but rather than advocating a return to Paradise Garden he called upon sleeping humanity to wake up and build 'with immense labours of the Imagination the fourfold London eternal',[2] city of art.

Emerson College, for all its concern for the natural environment, is not advocating a return to 'Noble Savagery'. 'Where man is not, nature is barren',[3] said Mr. Blake, and we would probably go along with that. We are indeed here to make marks upon the earth, but artistic marks which enhance what is given. We have tried, therefore, with limited financial resources, to apply the faculty of imagination to our surroundings, placing sculptural and architectural forms into the landscape, wild flowers on our tables. The college is no 'stately pleasure dome', but through care about the forms with which we surround ourselves (not all windows have 90° angles, for instance), and the substances that we use (wood, wool, transparent colours on the walls), we have managed to create a campus which speaks to the soul, beautiful as well as useful.

It has been an ideal of the college over the years that (rather than employing outside helpers) household tasks and care for the environment should play a part in the learning process, providing

Ruskin House

a testing ground for the heady things introduced in the classroom, and an opportunity to assimilate them. It also helps to keep the costs down.

## *Rock, flower, flesh and human heart*

We began the week by placing the stone, the plant, the animal (represented by the bronze dog) in front of us on our red carpet, and then one of us volunteered to sit amongst them as our human 'specimen'. Because it is fashionable nowadays to speak of the 'human animal', it was important for us to explore whether or not human presence added anything to the scene in front of us. We asked what each of the four things shared, and what their differences were. There were outward signs. The animal was not wearing clothes, but our human was. She could stand upright. She could articulate her thoughts, and (for some strange reason) she blushed when we talked about her. Outward signs for inner things? – for self-awareness. And as we talked further with her it emerged that she had a personal name and could remember she had raw carrots for lunch yesterday, and that she had an older sister on the other side of the Atlantic. She could have been fibbing, I suppose, but we believed her. She even claimed to have a biography and was imagining, and creatively planning, to be a midwife sometime in the future. After that we all joined in putting the dog on top of the stone, hiding it among the plant fronds, making its foot get trapped under a falling boulder and feeling sad about it. Kittens and puppies can be playful, I know, but only humans really play like that.

X 79. **Find a picture of someone, and take it as the focus of attention for an individual piece of writing, or for a written gossip with a partner. Or you could take a depiction of a group of people (see p.145) and explore in writing the quality of their interactions.**

X 80. **What (in one sentence) is a human being actually?**

- It is a creature who, thinking about this question, can say 'I don't know'.
- Humans, unlike dogs and cats, can woof one minute and miaow the next.
- A human is a being who can make decisions based upon past experience.
- A human being is a two-legged talking, self-conscious thinker.
- Humans know the names of things.

Here is Shakespeare's exploration of the question:

> What a piece of work is a man! How noble in reason! How infinite in faculty! In form and moving how express and admirable! In action how like an angel! In apprehension how like a god! The beauty of the world! The paragon of animals! And yet, to me, what is this quintessence of dust?[4]

## The fourfold human being

Having given some attention now to each of the 'queendoms' of nature, as my colleague John Davy liked to call them, it might be helpful to have them schematically before us, so that we can hold for a moment many thoughts in one thought. Here is another fourfold diagram (see also p.87), drawn from Rudolf Steiner's contribution on the subject:

| | | | | |
|---|---|---|---|---|
| * | * | * | Ego | *Fire* |
| * | * | Astral | Astral | *Air* |
| * | Etheric | Etheric | Etheric | *Water* |
| Physical | Physical | Physical | Physical | *Earth* |
| **Mineral** | **Plant** | **Animal** | **Human** | |

As the terminology may seem strange and unfamiliar, I will tease it out a little. The human being is seen here to have four 'bodies', including a potentially self-aware ego. The animal has three such bodies, being animated by the astral (desire) body. Its ego, not incarnated, works as a wise group-soul into all members of a particular species. The plant has two manifest bodies, a physical one and another that gives it life. The other two members work upon it peripherally. As for the mineral, its manifestation upon the earth is purely physical. That it has other, unmanifest bodies is harder for me to imagine, but there are people, more subtle-souled than I, who claim to sense the power that emanates from quartz or ruby. On the right side of the diagram the names of the four elements appear; they should again be understood as dynamic principles working within the various bodies. The fiery ego principle is what is celebrated in the Whitsun story that we will come to shortly. If you then consider what in your own being is stone-like (Earth), plant-like (Water), animal-like (Air), essentially human (Fire), you are likely to find yourself characterising aspects of the four humours or temperaments that were the basis of ancient physiology. Here, once again, we see the four elements at their essential work of bridging the gap between inner and outer experience.

## Our human dress

In the Grimm's fairy tale of *Allerleirau (Fur Skin)*,[5] we meet a princess who takes with her on her journey into the world three nuts with starry dresses hidden inside, disguising herself in a fourth garment patched together from the fur of every animal in the kingdom. There can be no definitive interpretation of such pictures, but I can't help feeling a resonance here with the imagination of the four 'bodies' that I have just described.

The story also alludes to the ancient understanding that the qualities and gestures found spread out, exaggerated and, brought to specialised perfection in the animal kingdom, are gathered together in the human being. We have noted already (see p.147) how this manifests in our constitution: what differentiates mammals into rodent, carnivore and ungulate finds in us humans (in nerve/sense, heart/lung, and metabolic/limb functions) a more balanced relationship, yet still allows almost endless individual variety.

These three different but interacting systems in our body provide the physical basis for our soul faculties of thinking, feeling and will respectively, which hopefully work harmoniously together.

If they do not (particularly in feeling life) then we soon resort to animal insults to express the difficulty, or animal fables in the attempt to remedy it.

If, on first acquaintance, this appears to be a hierarchical picture with the human being at the top and dominant, then this poem by Christian Morgenstern (reworked by me from various sources) provides a way of seeing it in a different light:

### The Washing of the Feet

Thank you, cold and silent stone;
I am bending here in awe before you.
From you the plant in me has grown.

And thanks to you, green leaf and flower;
I stoop in reverence before you.
You free in me the beast's quick power.

I thank you all, stone, plant and beast,
And bow in gratitude before you.
Your sacrifice gives me increase.

Receive our thanks, O child so bright.
This kneeling down in love before you
Means the Self may stand upright.

Thanks flows, and then in Love's command
Throughout the waiting world expands.
In thanks all Being joins its hands.[6]

*Christian Morgenstern*

The title refers, of course, to Christ's deed at the Last Supper when he knelt down to wash the feet of his disciples.

# *Whitsun: celebrating the human community*

At Emerson College we do celebrate (among others) the Christian festivals. In a community with such a mix of cultures and religions and non-religion we have the difficult and marvellous possibility of recreating our festivals in ways and words that are meaningful to each one of us, whatever our background.

The Whitsun festival (also known as Pentecost) belongs to this flowering time of the year, and sometimes it falls very conveniently into that moment when, in the writing group, we are turning our attention to what it means to be human. It has even been our task, some years, to prepare the event for the whole college, in which case we lay our pens aside and let our speech work come to prominence. Here is a slightly pruned version of the Bible story which provides the basis, fifty days after Easter, for this important festival:

And when the day of Pentecost was fully come they were all with one accord in the one place.

And suddenly there came a sound from heaven as of a rushing mighty wind, and it filled all the house where they were sitting.

And there appeared unto them cloven tongues as of fire, and it sat upon each of them.

And they were all filled with the Holy Ghost, and began to speak in other tongues as the Spirit gave them utterance.

Now when this was noised abroad, the multitude came together, and they were all amazed and marvelled, saying how hear we everyman in our own tongue, wherein we were born?

Parthians, and Medes, and Elamites, and the dwellers in Mesopotamia, and in Judea, and Cappadocia, in Pontus and Asia, Phrygia, and Pamphylia, in Egypt, and in the parts of Libya about Cyrene, and strangers in Rome, Jews and proselytes, Cretes and Arabians, we do hear them speak in our tongues the wonderful works of God.[7]

*from The Acts of the Apostles*

It is a fine story. Many would claim nowadays that that is all it is – 'a fairy tale', and nothing more. Others, while dismissing any historical or theological claim, would accept it as an imagination that has meaningful implications for our lives.

For Francis Edmunds, Whitsun was the festival which best embodied the spirit of this college that he founded – Japanese and Koreans, and Israelis, and the dwellers in Africa and the United States, in Chile and Brazil… – people of many tongues, religions and cultures, coming here to find a voice, to gather strength and skill, before going out to do creative work in farms and schools, families, communities and cities all over the world. In this festival we celebrate the free human spirit at work in community.

The garden of Pixton House

It was through Francis that I first understood this story to be the record of a turning point in the evolution of human consciousness. This was confirmed for me later through my reading of Owen Barfield who demonstrates a fundamental shift from an ancient inspirational culture in which the divine creative world still breathed its wisdoms through us, towards a new imaginative culture in which, through the power of that flame upon each brow, we begin to discover ourselves as free independent thinkers and creators.

If the Whitsun event does indeed mark the point at which we turned from creature-hood towards the realisation of our own creative potential then I am happy to celebrate it. Undoubtedly, something happened. Some fiery seed was planted around that time, and has been germinating since. How else can we explain the proliferation of books, such as this one, dedicated to the kindling of individual creativity?

## *Genius*

It is Owen Barfield's contention that the evolution of human consciousness leaves its traces (as a kind of fossil record) within our language. He observes, for instance, that the word 'enthusiasm', which originally implied possession by a God, now refers to a more inward creative source. The word 'genius' is another:

> … the history of poetic psychology is the story of a super-individual psychology, which extends from as far back as can be investigated up to at least the Renaissance, but with reverberations still going on much later; and which only then begins to be transformed into something like individual psychology. Then it becomes, or begins to become, a psychology of individual 'genius.' And so the word 'genius' changes its meaning. Originally the genius was a spirit-being, other than the poet himself; but that is not what we mean by genius today. The Romans would never have said of a man that he is a genius. They would have said he had, or was accompanied by, a genius. We prefer to say he is one.[8]

Here, in condensed form (and in my free rendering) is Rudolf Steiner's version of this story:

> The stars once spoke to us.
> It is world destiny
> That they are silent now.
> To be aware of that silence
> Can be pain for us here on Earth.
> But, as the silence deepens,
> There grows and ripens
> What we speak to the stars.
> To be aware of that speaking

Confirms us anew in spirit.[9]

## *What we speak*

Earlier I ventured that mineral is noun, flower is adjective, animal is verb, so I would add now the suggestion that all three come together in the human being as the living sentence. Some of us, of course, are more adjective-like, noun-like, or verb-like by nature, and perhaps each person's particular gift finds voice through one of them. All three, to some extent, have come to expression in our work together (see p.57), and the sounding and balancing of their qualities provides the basis for the speech work included in the course.

## *With one accord*

In the context of our work together I would say that the Whitsun story has provided me with the confidence that a circle of writers, 'with one accord in one place' (see p.185) can go into the silence and recreate language out of a deep attention to one another. This may be already apparent to you from the many collaborative writing tasks that we have done in response to the natural world. It can be deepened further by working together without any given subject matter:

X 81.  **Sit down quietly with someone and give your attention to them and to the place that you are sharing – to the turning point that is here and now. When you feel ready, and in 'one accord', begin a written conversation.**

Here is an example with a bit of the Whitsun wind blowing through it:

It's windier today. It clears my thoughts.

It sets the teasels nodding.

It pushes yesterday faster into tomorrow.

Yes, it is so hard to be here, now, when everything is moving past us.

I'll pull up my collar and try to stand in the moment.

Here, with these blue chairs. Now, with this afternoon light on our hands.

The wind will only forgive a moment. It is urging, insistent.

Forgive me for asking – but have you ever told me who you are, and why you are here, now, sharing this windy moment with me?

This is what I have to share: I am the one the wind pushes towards there and then.

There are the teasels nodding, and here you are, teasing me with enigmas.

For this moment, you are here and now. I will let the wind wait, and stand with you.

The blue chairs, I believe, are waiting for you to ask me a question.

When I reach tomorrow, then and there, will you still be here?

*PM with Peggy Rushton*

My impression is that in a written conversation the slowing down, the giving of time between responses, allows an element of ritual to come through, a communion in which word becomes bread, a sharing of substance. Zen masters and ancient Indian gurus used spoken dialogue as a sacred initiation technique. I am recommending the written conversation as a modern equivalent in which 'teacher' and 'student', creating out of nothing, are equally involved in the learning process. The word 'con-versation', by the way, is rooted in a sense of 'turning together'. Here is another example:

Birds don't sing much in the afternoons.

Yes, morning is the time for praise. Or are they claiming territory?

A meaningful claiming it is. I woke up before them, when it was still dark outside, when the only one claiming was the owl. Sometimes, even without me noticing, one single bird sounds and the next moment the space is full of their song. The shift it creates in me must belong to more than the claiming of territory.

To the ex-claiming of it, maybe. Each bird-type has a particular starting time, I'm told – its own moment and measure on the scale of dawn. The sun conducts the orchestra. Can you believe this?

Yes, I can. Or maybe most of all I wish to. The thought of a greater wisdom living in nature makes me feel supported somehow. And I believe the creatures that do not say 'I' have space for this wisdom to stream through them. Have you seen how flocks of birds shift direction in one moment, like each creature is a cell in one larger body?

More than seen! I have marvelled at it. Do I wish, then, to be a creature who doesn't say 'I' but only 'Ah' and 'Oh' as it hurls itself wholeheartedly across the sky? We used to be like that – building our territories with song. But now? We need guns and things. Do we have to give up being 'I'? Or can an 'I' praise in the morning?

Going from 'Ah' to 'I' created division. I think division led to fear, and that's when humans think they need 'guns and things'. My hope is that 'I' will keep going, will pass through the tunnel of fear. Because I think that something spectacular waits at the other end. I think there awaits a new way of seeing, and that the 'I' can choose to live in 'Ah' and 'I' at the same time.

*PM with Marte Tveter*

## Between You and Me

X 82.  Another version of this would be to write short letters back and forth while in the presence of the other person.

X 83.  As a further development, write a letter from one fictional person to another, then hand it to someone (preferably pre-decided upon) asking them to reply to it in the name and voice of the given character:

Dear Samuel,

I guess you have discovered by now that your green jumper is missing. Yes, it was me who took it. It was lying on the bed when I packed my rucksack and I don't think I hesitated even for a second before adding it on top of my own clothes. Maybe because by then it smelled more of me than of you. You know I was grateful to wear it on our cold morning walks though I never said anything when you handed it to me. I think you were pleased, too, quietly shivering in your too-thin shirt. I know it used to belong to your father, and if you really do mind I will wrap it up in brown paper for you to receive in the mail. Hope you are well, Kathleen.

Dear Kathleen,

I have noticed, of course. I noticed while you were packing it, in fact, but said nothing, feeling happy at the thought that you would still be wearing something of me when far away. I can imagine it now, your dear shape inside it, stretching it in ways I'd never be able to manage! I expect some flecks of grass still cling to it from that day we walked along the cliff top. Do you remember? After we had eaten our sandwiches we folded it very carefully and then we used it as a pillow, hardly big enough for the two of us, as we lay a long time on our backs, watching the small clouds passing. I am watching them now, but you are not here. Green was my father's favourite colour. Keep it until we meet next summer, Samuel.

*PM with Marte Tveter*

A fiction, yes, but sometimes you can sound more truly through an assumed per-sona. In choosing which fictional character to address, it would be good if the 'I' writing the first letter had a sense for some potential they wish to call forth in the 'You' who is to receive it. (Further ways of working socially with writing, and with the human ideals at the heart of language, can be found in my earlier book, *Sing Me the Creation*.)

## The turning point

The German poet, Rainer Maria Rilke describes in his poem 'The Turning Point', how one night, between sleep and waking, he experienced a conference going on in the air above his head. His early fame had rested on poems written out of the same close attention to things and plants and animals that we have been giving, but now the voices in the dark were saying that it was time for him write another kind of poetry:

> For to observation there is a limit, and the closely observed world wishes to blossom out in love. The work of the eyes is done, now do the heart's work on the impressions within you, the imprisoned impressions. For you mastered them; but now you do not know them. Behold, inner man, your inner bride, this creature won from a thousand beings, this creature merely won, never yet loved.[10]

We have met such a dichotomy before in what Coleridge had to say (see p.89) about the difference between his own poetic path and that of his friend, William Wordsworth.

The work of eyes connects more with Wordsworth's task:

> ... to give the charm of novelty to things of everyday, and to excite a feeling analogous to the supernatural, by awakening the mind's attention to the lethargy of custom, and directing it to the loveliness and the wonders of the world before us.

Heart work, on the other hand, is more along the lines of what Coleridge proposed for himself:

> ... directed to persons and characters supernatural, or at least Romantic; yet so as to transfer from our inward nature a human interest and a semblance of truth sufficient to procure for these shadows of imagination that willing suspension of disbelief for the moment, which constitutes poetic faith.[11]

In the end, I think, it is not a matter of choosing heart work over the work of the eyes. In writing about the things and creatures that inhabit the natural landscape, we have already found ourselves interpreting aspects of our own inner nature, moving freely back and forth between the two 'works' that Rilke refers to. Nevertheless, in taking up more directly the theme of how the human soul, 'the inner bride', can find expression, we reach a similar turning point. Soulscape rather than the given landscape will now become the focus of our attention, and persons supernatural will be our guides.

## Notes

1  Blake, W., *Complete Writings*, Oxford University Press, 1972, p.216
2  Ibid.
3  Ibid., p.152
4  Shakespeare, W., *Hamlet*, Act II, Scene II, Signet Classics, 1963, p.80
5  Grimm, J. and W., *The Complete Grimm's Fairy Tales*, Routledge and Keegan Paul, 1975, p.36
6  Morgenstern, M., *The Washing of the Feet*
7  *The Holy Bible*, Authorized Version, Acts of the Apostles, Ch.2
8  Barfield, O., *Speakers' Meaning*, Rupdolf Steiner Press, 1967, p.188
9  Steiner, R., *Verses and Meditations*, Rudolf Steiner Press, 1972, p.97
10  Rilke, R.M., in Bridgewater, P., (ed.) *Twentieth Century German Verse*, Penguin Books, 1963, p.41
11  Coleridge, S.T., *Biographia Literaria*, J.M. Dent & Co., 1906, Ch.13

# The Story We Belong To

*The study of a Grimm's fairy tale takes us more deeply now into realms of soul where the objects and creatures of the outer world serve as a language for our human inwardness, and the energy of the narrative becomes rhythmically patterned. In this context the practice of writing fictional letters is taken further. We then take up the task of writing our own soul story. A series of exercises in which the common matter of our biographies is transformed through fantasy, dream and play lead us towards the possibility of making up a story that is at the same time true. The question of how imagination can serve the truth naturally comes back again.*

## Fairy-tale

In the 18th and 19th centuries, all over Europe, the Romantic poets, intent on finding 'the real language of men', went around collecting ballads, supposedly created by pre-literate Noble Savages (see p.51 and p.151). If they could not find any they made them up. If they did find some they often polished and 'improved' them. The same impulse inspired the Brothers Grimm in Germany to do their painstaking work of collecting the Household Tales (or 'Fairy Stories', as we call them) that folk still passed on from mouth to mouth.[1] Whatever re-creation took place as they wrote them down was absorbed and included in the living tradition of story-making.

We can ask what such stories are made of. First of all it should be said that their beginnings and endings are very particular. Here are some of the ways in:

- When I was a lad and so was my dad.
- In olden times when wishing still helped one.
- In the thrice ninth land in the thrice tenth kingdom.
- Once upon a time, when pigs spoke rhyme,
  And monkeys chewed tobacco,
  And dogs took snuff to make them tough
  And ducks went quack quack quack-O.[2]

These (like the exercises in this book) are intended to act as spells to usher our consciousness across from the world of sense to the world of soul. Time and space are deliberately confounded. *East of the Sun and West of the Moon*, is another example – a seemingly silly place, and yet every month, between full moon rising and setting sun, we can find ourselves there. Dogs don't take snuff, maybe, but ducks do say quack-O. These magic formulae, often in verse form, alert us to the fact that the imaginal world is differently constituted and speaks a different language.

## Little Snow White

The story of 'Little Snow White' has been alluded to throughout this book. Here is the beautiful way in which it begins:

> Once upon a time in the middle of winter, when the flakes of snow were falling like feathers from the sky, a queen sat at a window sewing, and the frame of the window was made of black ebony. And whilst she was sewing and looking out of the window at the snow, she pricked her finger with the needle, and three drops of blood fell upon the snow. And the red looked pretty upon the white snow, and she thought to

herself, would that I had a child as white as snow, as red as
blood, and as black as the wood of the window-frame. Soon
after that she had a little daughter, who was as white as snow,
and as red as blood, and her hair was as black as ebony, and
she was therefore called little Snow-white. And when the child
was born, the queen died.[3]

At this point it would be good to turn to the Appendix (p.240)
and read the whole story, becoming familiar enough with it to be
able to:

X 84.   **Recreate the story from memory around the group,
adding no reflections about it on the way. Anything left
out in the telling can be added afterwards. I am taking
this story as a model, but feel free to choose another more
suited to your culture or purpose.**

To safeguard us from rushing headlong into analysis of the tale I
suggest that first we let our hands do the talking:

X 85.   **Explore through a pastel drawing the dynamics of black,
white, red, that feature so strongly.**

The story begins with a queen sewing beside an open window.
This opening becomes, momentarily, a way in to the pre-birth
world, and a vision is granted of the child who will come to her.
Black and red and white – they are described as physical attributes;
but an imaginative reader will readily sense that these are outward
signs of the threefold stitch-work, body, soul and spirit, that
constitutes every human being coming into the world. Nor is this
any abstract notion. We can even employ these aspects of ourselves
to bring us, step by step, closer to an understanding of the story:

**Step one (black):** Having faithfully recreated the body of the story, we can frame its basic facts – how the different kingdoms of nature to which we have given so much attention make their appearance here:

- the things – window, needle, mirror, candles, comb, laces, coffin, iron shoes.
- the plants – forest, apple, tree root.
- the animals – bear, owl, raven, dove.
- the human characters – queens, king, Snow White, huntsman, dwarves, prince.

Those are the facts in space. In the realm of time and relationship, we can note how the number three keeps reoccurring – three drops of blood, three colours, three trials, three birds on the glass coffin, even the fact that there are three glass objects in the story. Then there is the number seven – seven dwarves, seven hills that the wicked queen has to cross on the way to their house. Questions begin to arise (you might recognize this as belonging to the second step of the fourfold process that we worked with earlier, see p.106).

## X 86. Write a list of questions that arise in you through reading the story:

> How did those three drops of blood get onto the snow?
> Why did one dwarf spend an hour in each of the other dwarves' beds?

**Step two (red):** We can look now at how the story moves us, stirs our blood. We soon come to realise that this is no realm of dumb dead things, but a speaking world, where mirrors answer back, where even the numbers and colours articulate qualities of soul.

That an owl, a raven and a dove visit the dead Snow White in turn, and in precisely that order, feels like language to me. Three birds. Three trials. We adult readers, expecting information to be spoken once and clearly, might feel these repeated patterns to be rather tiresome.   For the children, however (especially if they themselves are too tight laced), this is healing fare. They breathe with what is rhythmically in formation there, and sigh deeply when the happy ending comes. We may also have some qualms about the witch being forced to dance to death in red hot iron shoes. But remember – this is soul country, where the things of the outer world mirror our inwardness. What better way to transform a cold heart than to put fire below (see p.85) and get some iron dancing through it?

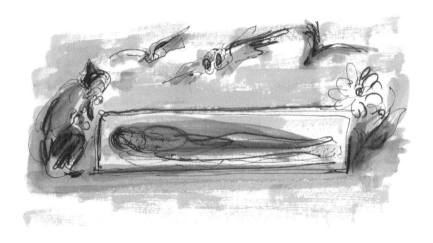

X 87.  **At this point we can give scope to a more psychological exploration of the story:**

The queen had nothing against her step-daughter. The girl was colourless, like light, she could come into a room and you'd look through her. The queen had a proper sense of her own beauty. When she walked into a room she commanded people's attention, lifted them out of the concerns of their daily lives. At night, or at dangerous times of the month, mid-cycle usually, when the moon was very full, images of her step-daughter rose in her mind and hung like mist around a thorny tree: white as snow, red as blood and black as ebony. She tried to push the images away. The girl was colourless after all, in essence, whereas she was the substance of cream and roses, cream of the rose, mistress of all she touched with her hand or her foot. Moreover, she had an eye that could see, as they say, without spectacles. It knew, did the eye, what was lacking, told her what it was that people wanted, and all that was wanted became itself in her. They called her the Queen of Hearts. She broke hearts. ('Taste the fruit,' she said, 'the red part is good, isn't that what you wanted?')...

She described her step-daughter as the proverbial ray of sunshine – except that the girl was wet. What she meant was, the people loved the girl and she never had to work at it. She could sit in a room – the Queen watched her – stroking the dog, doing her embroidery or nothing at all (how beautifully she did that) and saw how something breathed from her and settled like dew on everyone around her. They felt revived without knowing why. Something in them lifted up like wilting flowers do after a soft rain. She was born like it. Naturally good, like her mother, the people said, and the Queen saw no virtue in that. She herself had worked all her life to become the best she could possibly be. Hard work she could respect wherever she found it. Natural goodness left her un-moved...

*Andie Lewenstein*

This is the first part of a longer piece. Writing about it, Andie (who has been my collaborator in this work with story) says:

It draws on the original Grimm's fairy tale, assumes a familiarity with the story and has one foot there and the other in contemporary, post-Freudian consciousness. It uses third person narrative from the viewpoints of both queen and Snow White – and a narrator who stands both inside and outside the story. Many people find this way of 'retelling' a creative way of exploring political and/or moral questions as well as a powerful and dynamic way of addressing personal issues.

*Andie Lewenstein*

**X 88.** **Another way to do this is through first person monologue in which the characters or objects express their feelings (and interpret yours) about the story in which they find themselves.**

Here is a piece which picks up on the theme of the testing of innocence:

### The Apple Speaks:

Poison; yet I too was made good. The queen pulled me down. Snow White took me only to her throat. For the power of me she could not breathe. She fell into a deep sleep. She could not take me into her vast whiteness. The seven guards wept, yet did believe.

The prince's kiss brought me back up. As I withdrew she awakened. But, I liked to be in her, to take her consciousness, to test if she could hold her self with me. Yes, I was made good, but now I can taste this fallen desire and find too clean her whiteness.

*Triena Wing*

**The third step (white):** It would be too crass to ask, 'What does the story mean?', yet at this stage of the process we cannot avoid a question that children carry – 'Is it a true story?' As modern adults, how can we tell such stories if we can't answer them truly? Could there, for instance, have been six dwarves instead of seven? This is spirit work, though in attempting it we face the same dilemma that the scientist has when facing the plant – 'Must I kill the thing in order to fully grasp its laws?' The clear light of the intellect that we have won for ourselves since the Greeks 'invented' it cannot avoid such trials on its way to further transformation. Isn't this what the story itself tells us? – that Little Snow White must be tested in brain and breast and belly, and actually die in the process before, stumbling on a tree root, a resurrection comes (see p.248).

There must be countless psychological, spiritual, feminist, sociological, interpretations of 'Snow White and the Seven Dwarves', as we call it in England – and the wonderful thing is that the story accepts them all, and is great enough not to be measured or reduced by them.

As for me, on different days I see it different ways. For sure, it brings us news about our own soul's journey. Right now, I'm interested in the relation here between truth and beauty, and why pretty combs and ribbons offered to the senses are not to be trusted.

> We are led to believe in a lie
> When we see with and not through the eye.[4]

That is what Blake says. Is this what 'Innocence' has to learn? – that it must fall into the sense world to win beauty out of 'Experience'? Shut here in our glass coffins, we are only able to say, 'beauty is in the eye of the beholder'. All is vanity.

In this book, however, I am proposing a conscious path of imagination whereby we might eventually come to say with the English poet, Kathleen Raine, that 'Beauty is the aspect of things loved'.[5] Love, taken up into the act of perception, shows us a way (beyond subjectivity and objectivity) into a new, yet ancient, way of apprehending the beautifying principle that created this world; of finding Rilke's 'inner bride' (see p.193) who makes her appearance at the end of the story.

I am trying (too hard, perhaps) to forge a connection here between the looking glass in the queen's bedroom and this theme that I keep returning to of beauty-in-truth, of truth-in-beauty. The story itself is beautiful, but is it a true one? 'A semblance of truth?' (see p.193) I live in questions. Let's try it another way:

X 89.   Write fictional letters again, but this time choosing a character from the fairy tale. Give it to someone else in the group and ask them to reply to it, finding the voice of the character they have been given to embody:

Dear Mirror,

You were not always mine. You belonged to the dead queen. I inherited you. I suppose you spoke to her, too. Or perhaps she was so confident about her beauty that she never asked. You must've felt rather empty in the days after she died. And then there I was, standing before you, wondering whether I could ever fill the gap that her beauty had left behind. Beauty. I live for beauty. So much of my days I spend combing my hair in front of you. The dead queen liked embroidery, I'm told; but I can't believe she had the passion I have for pretty laces and things. I'm more beautiful than she ever was – I'm sure I am.

Please tell me I am. I was gazing into you the other day when I saw little Snow White reflected there behind me. A fear gripped my heart. I had a feeling that your cold surface melted a little to see her smiling there. What is it about her, I wonder, that you can't find in my own queenly radiance? The old queen is in her coffin. A glass coffin awaits Snow White on the mountainside. As for me – I have a glass thing, too. Please, dear Mirror, don't be the coffin into which my beauty dies.

Dear Queen,

Thank you for your letter. You are right. I was not always yours, but I am delighted to belong to you. Might I add – I never belonged to the dead queen, for whoever looks into me has to be alive. When they die they then become part of me, reflecting whoever is destined to look. Brave hearts always, I might add.

The last queen also spoke to me, but she asked more about truth than beauty. Her kingdom was riddled with lies. It is true, her love for embroidery and her beauty – that was astounding, but she was impenetrable. That was why, eventually, that needle had to prick her finger. Unlike you she had no passion at all. Her heart was not as brave as yours; that's why her child is pale and weak, even if beautiful. Do you really want that kind of beauty?

Oh passionate queen, can you not see my answers to your questions are made to taunt you? To drive your will to hunt Snow White yourself. To test her, to challenge her yourself. Don't be like the old queen who sat all day at the window. Don't send huntsmen to do your task. Leave the castle; disguise yourself; be the angel to give to Snow White what her mother could never fulfil. For you are the Passionate Redeemer. No one is as passionate as you, but you only asked who is the fairest of us all.

When you die I shall rejoice at no longer being a cold mirror. Snow White will have to look into the warm light to ask her question. I wonder what question that will be.

With love, the Mirror.

*PM with Luci Sale*

## What the matter is

In these last pages we have been engaging with one of the high stories pertaining to the progress of the human soul, rhythmically patterned, and set apart (beyond the seven hills) from the common matter of our lives. If we are to go there in our own writing (and we will take that as an aim) then it would be good to take into account what W.B. Yeats has to say in his poem, 'The Circus Animals' Desertion':

> Those masterful images because complete
> Grew in pure mind, but out of what began?
> A mound of refuse or the sweepings of the street,
> Old kettles, old bottles, old rags, that raving slut
> Who keeps the till. Now that my ladder's gone,
> I must lie down where all the ladders start,
> In the foul rag-and-bone shop of the heart.[6]

We will lead, then, this basic matter (mother stuff) of our lives – together with their accompanying fears, joys, sorrows, longings, memories, dreams – into a lively intercourse with the patterning (paternal) power of the imagination, and thereby fructify the words for the telling of our own soul story.

## Fabulous memories

X 90. **Write a list of memories (sentences rather than paragraphs), starting each one with 'I remember', or 'I'll never forget'.**

> I remember how our voices echoed in the public swimming pool. I remember discovering the stolen handbag under the Rhododendron bush. I remember the big girls next door mocking me because I did not know my two times table. I remember the butterflies in Richard Truelove's garden…

X 91. **Develop one or more of those memories into a written anecdote. Biography has always been prime stuff for writers to draw from:**

> When I was five we lived in my Grandmother's house. Just opposite was a block of flats where my friend Richard Truelove lived. The buddleias in his back garden seemed always filled with butterflies. When my cousin and I went over to play we clapped our hands over those butterflies and didn't mind that they died, because the powder from their wings left such lovely colours on our fingers. One day a boy called Bill who lived down the road got very angry with us and chased us around that garden with a brick in his hand. We all ran different directions. I ran around the side of the big house, down a narrow alleyway. Then I saw Bill with his brick coming

Butterflies in the buddleia

the other way. He raised his hand and was just about to kill me when a window beside us was suddenly flung open and the person inside said 'Boys, what are you making all this noise for?' Bill put down his brick, and I ran home to my mother, glad to be alive.

*PM*

Notice that we have begun to use a lot of personal names in the writing. The beginning of 'Little Snow White' gives us an example of how a name comes to a person.

## X 92. Tell the story of your name (another way of drawing upon biographical matter).

If an example is needed, I must bring one from my own life, I suppose, yet find myself strangely hesitant as I do so. My first two names are Paul Michael: Michael, because I was born on Michaelmas day, and because my uncle Michael had been killed at Dunkirk; Paul, because during the air-raids over London my mother, pregnant with me, sheltered in the crypt of St. Paul's Cathedral. I like that story; it is something of the myth of me – to be twice sheltered within the building that I was later to be named after. Anyone who has had the responsibility of naming a child will know the depth of intuition required. What instance of putting a word in its right place could be more intimate than this? My shyness at the beginning of this paragraph probably arises out of some sense for it.

## X 93. Give one of your written anecdotes to someone and ask them to metamorphose the personal matter of it towards the pattern of fairy tale. The aim is not to dismiss or sentimentalise the facts, but to enhance their meanings or hidden gestures:

Once upon a time there was a boy who lived with his grandmother in a small hut just outside the palace walls. He could see the tops of the trees in the royal garden tossing in the wind, and he did so long to be there. Soon he found a way to climb up that wall and into the garden where he spent many a happy hour playing among the flowers. His special delight was to watch the brightly coloured butterflies fluttering from blossom to blossom among the buddleias. Sometimes in his joy he clapped his hands and if a butterfly happened to get caught between his hands and die there, well he did not mind so very much because the powder from their wings left such pretty colours on his fingers. One day a bull who usually lived safely in a paddock nearby broke its fence down and, attracted by the bright colours on the boy's shirt and hands, came charging towards him. The boy cried out. Butterflies fluttered away in all directions. He ran around the side of the palace and thought that he had escaped from that bull when suddenly there it was, coming towards him down the alleyway. There was no time to turn back. He thought his last moment had come. Suddenly a window in the palace flew up and there stood the King who called out, 'What is the cause of this rumpus in my garden?' The bull reared up in astonishment, giving just enough time for the boy to turn on his heels and run back to the hut where his grandmother lived. When he told her the story she said, 'If you truly love those butterflies you should not harm them.'

*Michael Forster*

Perhaps this sense that our lives are rhythmic and artistic stories, and that we are active in the composition of them, is already a reality for you. The Scottish poet, Edwin Muir, was not in doubt of it:

There are times in every man's life when he seems to become for a little while a part of the fable, and to be recapitulating some ancient drama.[7]

The American poet, Robert Duncan, says it even more explicitly:

In the light of the mythological, events and persons can seem true or false to the true story of who I am.[8]

Here (my transformation of the animal anecdote on p.138) is another example:

One day a little girl was playing happily in her garden when she slipped on the mossy path and grazed her shin. As she was sitting there she saw that the wound was bleeding. It did hurt a little, but really it was the sight of the red blood that made her burst into tears. There she sat sobbing and nobody, it seemed, could hear her. Just then she heard a whirring close to her ear, and a small green fly came down and settled right on her bleeding shin. The sight of that brilliant green against the bright red of her blood was so startling that somehow the little girl forgot to cry. 'Hello, little fly,' she said. 'Where do you come from?' The fly said nothing. But it did begin to move, up and down the length of that red graze on her skin. The red blood stopped its flowing. Any pain that the little girl had was melting away. She heard her mother calling from the top of the path. 'Here I am, mother,' the girl replied, and as she turned her head to do so she saw a flash of green and heard that whirring sound again close to her ear. 'Are you alright,' asked her mother? 'No, no, I've hurt myself! Look,' said the girl. She looked. They both looked. There was no wound to be seen. 'Oh, you are alright,' said her mother; and the girl went back to her playing. Was it a dream? She never saw that green fly again.

*PM*

In doing this we are, in effect, opening our night eye within our daytime consciousness. We have seen how the poet, Rilke, in his poem 'The Turning Point', received important instruction through his attention to the space between these two realms (see p.192). On our path of imagination we, too, need to touch into this twilight zone a little.

# *Day dreaming*

X 94.  Make two columns – one for night, one for day – and
write words into them (or gather some from the group)
which characterise their qualities:

|              | NIGHT        | DAY          |
|--------------|--------------|--------------|
|              | Unconscious  | Conscious    |
|              | Soft         | Sharp        |
|              | Female       | Male         |
|              | Periphery    | Centre       |
|              | Together     | Separate     |
|              | Moon         | Sun          |
|              | Eternity     | Time         |
|              | Wisdom       | Knowledge    |
|              | Poetry       | Philosophy   |
|              | Flow         | Form         |
|              | Matter       | Pattern      |

We could go on a long time polarising them in this way, but my
aim here is to assume Mercury's role of coaxing these contraries
into some creative dialogue:

X 95.  Make up a short dream narrative. Each person in the
circle write one word (a concrete noun would be best) on
a small piece of paper, fold it, and pass it to the left. On a
larger page (each person their own) now begin a dream
story, two sentences at the most, into which the received
word is incorporated. When everyone is ready, pass the
words on again, and continue the same story, introducing
the new word. The moment of giving the word away and
then receiving it is important and should be done with

**ceremony, surrendering (as in sleep) to chaos and the unknown, then waking to what word the day unfolds:**

A woman with an <u>umbrella</u> was walking along the path. Under her left arm she was carrying a purple <u>cushion</u>. She was being very careful not to let any rain fall on that cushion. Ah, but was it really a cushion? No – it was a loaf of <u>bread</u> shaped like a baby. The woman was being very careful not to let any rain fall on that <u>baby</u>. At the end of the path there was a <u>beehive</u>, and the woman stopped and listened to the bees buzzing inside it. She bent down and in a sing song voice said, 'Please bees give some <u>rose petal</u> honey to my baby'.

And:

There was a bowl of <u>raspberries</u> on the table. A small <u>bird</u> flew in through the window and started pecking at them. I was saving those berries for my <u>friend</u>, but then I thought maybe this bird is a friend. It was a speaking bird which said 'I am a blackbird'. It sounded like '<u>blackboard</u>', though; and suddenly I was in a classroom with a map of the <u>world</u> on the wall. All its oceans were the colour of raspberry juice. It was dripping off the edges of the map into some <u>cups</u> on the floor below. My friend likes juice, I thought. I will give it to him as a <u>present</u> when he comes.

*Leahcim Retsrof*

This is one playful way to bridge the gap between day and night, daring like Joseph (that great dreamer in the Bible)[9] to wear our many-coloured pyjamas in the daytime. Conversely, another essential practice on this path of imagination would be to carry something of our day-time awareness with us into sleep.

# *Seeing in the dark*

In ancient times the temple acted as the mediator between these two realms. Nowadays we are free to do it out of our own contemplations, and we do not have to go very far to find the beginnings of such a practice. It is a common experience that our random or inconclusive thoughts before bedtime can emerge miraculously patterned and coherent in the morning. It is only a matter, then, of taking hold of this and consciously offering up our questions into the night. And will the answer be there in the morning? Not necessarily; but if you are attentive during the day then some chance meeting, or a book you happen to take off the shelf, may bring you one. Another way of offering something up before you go to sleep is (by Rudolf Steiner's recommendation[10]) to call to mind, in backwards order and without judgement, the events and images of the day. The night self cannot make much use of finished things, it seems; but through the effort involved in such a backwards review we release the effects of the day back to the creative realm, to their causes (where our dream self dwells), asking what can be made of them.

> I have a little brain
> Tucked safely in my head
> And another little brain
> Which is in the air instead
> This follows me, and plays with me
> And talks to me in bed
> The other one confuses me,
> The one that's in my head.[11]

*Annabel Laurence, age 10*

According to the Roman poet, Virgil, true dreams come to us from the gates of Horn, false ones through the gates of Ivory. My theory on this is that ivory, being connected to the teeth and digestive system, admits those dreams which image the many goings on of our intestines, whereas horn (connected to the head) indicates the possibility of a less clouded insight. Michaelangelo surely had that in mind when he depicted Moses with a pair of horns. Anyway, a common feature of dreams, whatever gate they slip through, is that they spin the daytime matter of our lives into symbolic images. Flying and chaotic, the strands are; but just sometimes (especially if we have practised the backwards review for a while) a sequence will come to us so extraordinarily patterned that we suspect some wisdom working behind their fabric. It might be in the form of a coherent dream image. It might (as it was with Coleridge, see p.90) be in the form of words. Here are some words I was given:

> You breathe in as kingdom;
> You breathe out as air.
> Your kingdom is everywhere.[12]

It could have been 'heir', of course. It could have been 'Aire'. A master of word-play this Dreamer is, intent on inner and outer, centre and periphery, breathing together.

## Words at play

Friedrich Schiller expresses the view that most of the time we are bound – either by the laws of logic, or by natural necessity. Only in play, he says, can we be free from them, or free to balance their one-sided tyrannies: 'Man is fully human only when he plays, and he only plays when he is human in the fullest sense of the word.'[13] The practice of art, beauty-making, is a further development of this play principle – yet another manifestation of Mercury holding the creative balance between the fixity or chaos that the four elements, by themselves, are prone to (see p.27 and p.87). Here are a few story games to stir his quicksilver:

X 96.   Everyone put a folded word (or two if it is a small group) into a hat. Stir a story into it, then each take a word. Now tell a brief story round the circle, introducing your received word into it when your turn comes. Afterwards you can retell it in a more flowing manner.

X 97.   Make up some 'tiny tales' in which person, place, action, are immediately present. Try to write pure narrative, leaving out the sentiment for now. Nursery rhymes often provide good examples:

Jack and Jill
Went up the hill
To fetch a pail of water;
Jack fell down
And broke his crown
And Jill came tumbling after.

You can do it in the Diamond form described on p.83:

Leona
is old
and always sleeps
in a
corner.

Here are some more, though I have shaped them differently:

• Sally skipped gaily as she sucked her green lolly.
• My friend Jack opened a bottle of bright sadness.

- John opened his front door and ran down to the end of the world.
- Ramon bought a guitar and plucked the strings in a park where nobody could hear him.

X 98.   The Interrupter game is fun to play. Sit with a partner and begin to make up a simple story. Your partner's role is to throw in random words from time to time – *Candle*, *Elbow*, *Peanut* – and you must immediately incorporate them into the unfolding story. The partner can also say, 'No it didn't', and you must agree and change the narrative accordingly. After about five minutes of that you can change roles.

X 99.   Try again the exercise of receiving words from the group into your ongoing writing, but this time let it be more in fairy-tale mode:

Once upon a time there was a boy called Jack. He was walking along a path, just <u>humming</u> to himself, when he met his <u>sister</u>, Jill, coming the other way. Where are you going Jack, said Jill. I'm looking for gold, said Jack. Gold, said Jill. There's nothing <u>golden</u> to be found along this path. You never know, said Jack, and on he went. He licked his finger, then lifted it in the air to see which way the wind was blowing. It was blowing the same way that he was walking. This encouraged him, and he began to hum even more merrily than before. It was a <u>song</u> that his mother had taught him – and as he was singing it with his nose in the air he felt something sharp under his heel. He bent down and looked at it. It was a <u>nail</u>. Not just any old nail – but a golden nail, gleaming in the morning sunlight. 'Well, sister Jill,' he whispered cheekily. 'What did I tell you?' But Jill – she was too far away to hear him.

*Michael Forster*

Here at Emerson College we do have a School of Storytelling, and I am sure that my colleagues there could endlessly expand on this repertoire of story games.

## *Happily ever after?*

Now that you are familiar with the soul's topography you could:

X 100. **Make up your own introductory spell (see p.78) to carry us 'over the seven hills to where the seven dwarves dwell'.**

X 101. **Compose your own first paragraph of a fairy tale, including person, place and action:**

> Once, when was it, when wasn't it, there was a boy called Jack. So poor he was that he was delighted one morning to find a silver penny lying on his doorstep. But, being not only poor, but also honest, he knew that the coin must surely belong to somebody and so, saying a quick goodbye to his mother, he set off down the road to find out who that somebody could be, and as he walked he threw that silver penny up into the air and caught it again, and every time he did so it sparkled in the morning sunlight.
>
> *Michael Forster*

X 102. **Give your first paragraph to another person, asking them to provide the second, and back to you, following the yarn towards an ending waiting to be discovered.**

Having led the personal matter of our lives through the patterning craft inherent in fantasy, dream and collaborative play, it is time now to:

X 103. **Write, in fairy tale form, the story that belongs to you.**

This task is a difficult one for modern people. Apart from the fact that castles and princesses no longer belong to our immediate experience our modern consciousness is one which separates meaning from image. Since Freud, Jung, and others did their pioneering work we know all the psychological interpretations of such 'symbols'. The traditional tales, however, emerged out of a consciousness which *thought* in pictures. Certainly those pictures are filled with wisdoms, but those wisdoms cannot be extracted from the image without reducing its meaning. The image is not the meaning in disguise – it is its revelation. All too often, modern attempts at fairy-story make us feel that we are being preached at from beneath the surface.

Beware, then, of mapping it out too consciously. Give yourself to the images as you work, and the story that unfolds is sure to bear the footprint of your own soul's journey. Patterns and potentials, previously veiled, may be revealed, and healing brought to painful situations through the objectifying pictures that the realms of mineral, plant and animal provide. A colleague who has taken this aspect of the work further is Nancy Mellon. Her book, *The Art of Storytelling*,[14] supplements what I have only been able to touch upon here.

We have already considered (see p.196) the formulae which help us cross the threshold into such stories. Similarly, at the end, they give us the means to make our exit graciously:

- They lived happily ever after.
- They lived long and died happy,
  And never drank out of a dry cappy.
- And I know it is true, because a friend of mine was at the wedding, and she gave me a piece of the cake.

# The patterns in matter

Having gone through the looking-glass into the world of soul and the supernatural, we emerge once more into the light of day. Perhaps, though, we find that the light has a subtlety to it previously unnoticed. G.K. Chesterton (writing at the beginning of the 20th century) is especially helpful in pointing out how the patterns of fairy tale can transform our relationship to the everyday matter of our lives:

> Of all forms of literature, it seems to me, fairy tales give the truest picture of life. There may be errors in detail, but in a world so full of strange things they scarcely matter. Two-headed giants and beanstalks that climb up into the sky may not be true, but assuredly they are not too wonderful to be true. But the atmosphere of the fairy tale is astonishingly true to life. It deals with the silent witchery that lies in common things, corn and stones and apple trees and fire. It presents these, no doubt, as magic stones and magic apple trees, and if anyone will stare at them steadily in a field at twilight, he will find himself quite unable to assert that they are not magic. Let me take one quite practical example of the truth of fairy tales. In these stories success is made to depend upon a number of small material objects and observances; life is a chain of talismans. If a man touches three trees in passing, he is safe; if he touches four, he is ruined. If the hero meets a miller without a beard, he is to answer none of his questions. If he plucks a red flower in a particular meadow, he will have power over the mighty kings of some distant city. Now this poetic sense of the decisiveness of some flying detail is a thousand times more genuine and practical than the pompous insistence on some moral or scientific law which is the basis of most realistic novels. None of us know when we have done something

irrevocable. Our fate has been often decided by the twist of a
road or the shape of a tree. Nay, it has often been decided by
an omnibus or an advertisement, and there can therefore be
little reason for denying that it is a magic omnibus or a magic
advertisement.[15]

A 'magic advertisement'? Here is something I wrote when the logo
for our local supermarket happened to provide just the right
message to save me from a dark mood:

> I went down to the end of the lane, crossed the small stream,
> and started to climb the hill behind our house.
>
> Usually I enjoy that walk, but today it seemed dank and paltry.
>
> When I reached the edge of the Forest
> I glanced back into the valley to see how small my life was.
>
> A white plastic bag was hanging from a branch above my head.
>
> The writing on its side said, 'We are open whenever you need us'.
>
> *PM*

As for the magic 'omnibus', I recently received this message from
Australia:

> A few weeks ago I was in Sydney for one day. In that one day I
> rode one bus. I got on it and the driver said to me, 'No, no, this
> isn't your bus, you need to be on <u>that</u> one' – and pointed to
> another bus with exactly the same number on it. He was very
> adamant, so I said ok, got off his bus and stepped on to the one
> he indicated only to find a dear friend of mine sitting smack in
> front of the door! We hugged and cried in disbelief, and I'm

sure the driver was some messenger in disguise with special angelic duties. My heart sings for these moments and something settles into a much larger embrace.

*Liat Sokal*

These are both examples of those times when a bigger pattern (the 'fable' of who we are) touches in to the matter of our lives. Yes, the fairy tales bring news – that our individual biographies are patterned meaningfully – and how deeply children listen to these living pictures, gaining confidence for the day when they too will be tested.

In the great myths and scriptures of the world we can, with a little imagination, discern the same thing happening with the larger, historical story that we belong to. The Whitsun story (see p.185) is a good example of this. 'Myth', says Kathleen Raine, 'is the truth of fact'.[16]

# *Notes*

1   Grimm, J. and W., *Household Tales*, trans. by Hunt, M., George Bell, 1884
2   Jacobs, J., (ed.) *English Fairy Tales*, Dover Publications inc., 1967, p.68
3   Grimm, J. and W., *Household Tales*, trans. by Hunt, M., George Bell, 1884
4   Blake, W., *Complete Writings*, Oxford University Press, 1972, p.433
5   Raine, L., 'A Sense of Beauty' in *Resurgence*, Issue 114, Jan/Feb 1986
6   Yeats, W.B., *Collected Poems*, Macmillan & Co. Ltd., 1960, p.361
7   Muir, E., *Autobiography*, Cannongate Books, 1993
8   Duncan, R., *The Truth and Life of Myth*, The Sumac Press, 1968, p.8
9   *The Holy Bible*, Authorized Version Genesis, Ch.37, verses 3 and 23
10  Steiner, R., *An Outline of Occult Science*, Anthroposophic Press, 1972, p.291

[11] Lewis, R., (ed.) *Miracles*, Simon and Schuster, 1966, p.164
[12] Matthews, P., *The Ground that Love Seeks*, Five Seasons Press, 1996, p.106
[13] Schiller, F., *The Aesthetic Education of Man*, Frederick Unger Publishing Co., 1965, letter 15
[14] Mellon, N., *The Art of Storytelling*, Element Books, 1998
[15] Chesterton, G.K., *The Man Who was Orthodox*, A.P. Watt and Son
[16] Raine, K., *Defending Ancient Springs – 'On the Mythological'*, Oxford University Press, 1967

*College buildings & pylon from the Medway bridge*

# Walking Back the Way We Came

*The value of a review to conclude our work together is emphasised. Fundamental themes are recalled, and 'the practice of between-ness' enlarged upon. An example is given of how the review process can be absorbed into writing. Some sort of ceremonial closing before disbanding is essential, and the group might wish to do this by sharing the fruits of its work with a wider audience.*

One of my early mentors in nature observation, Fritz Julius, recommended that when you go for a walk you should walk back the same way as you came. Strange advice; but I have since realised that there is wisdom in looking at both sides of a thing, and that this can be applied fruitfully to activities other than walking. When you come to the end of a writing course, for instance, it is most important to spend time recapitulating and recollecting, otherwise the energy that has been generated leaks away. Our last week began, therefore, with naming the details of what we had done. The Contents page of this book, and the summaries at the beginning of each 'Week', are my own attempt to include something of an on-going review process, so I will not reiterate it here, but in ruminating over the various spells that you have chosen to work with, and the pieces you have written, you will find that what began as ideas becomes more deeply grounded in your being. Remember what the little boy said (see p.146): 'The cow does not eat much, but what it eats it eats twice so that it gets enough' – there seems to be some wisdom in that foolishness.

# *Re-membering*

It would also be important to remember the aims of our work – why, exactly, have we been doing this? Here is a sonnet by the 19th century French poet, Gerard de Nerval, which could help us:

**Golden Lines**

*What! Everything is sentient! (Pythagoras)*

Man, free thinker! Do you believe yourself the one alone thinking
in this world where life bursts forth in everything?
Your free will disposes of the forces that you hold
But in all your councils the universe is absent.

Respect in the animal an active intellect:
Each flower is a soul in nature bloomed forth;
A mystery of love lies concealed in the metal;
"Everything is sentient!" Everything has power over your being.

Beware in the blind wall a gaze that watches you:
To the very matter a spoken word is in-bound.
Do not make it serve some impious use.

Often in the obscure being dwells a hidden God;
And like a nascent eye covered by its lids
A pure spirit grows beneath the skin of stones.[1]

*Tr. Robert Duncan*

It seems to me that Nerval (madman? initiate poet?) gathers into these fourteen lines an essence of all the themes that we have worked with:

- He names the four realms of nature – mineral, plant, animal and human – that have centrally occupied our attention.
- He characterises for us the nature of modern western consciousness which has achieved its freedom at the expense of being able to participate in the life and innate intelligence of the world it contemplates.
- He makes an urgent call for a new reverential consciousness which can include the universe (a holistic approach) in its considerations of the natural world.
- He uses the word 'in' eight times in the poem.
- He implies that an intelligent being spoke this world into existence, and that each creature holds within it an essence of the word (meaning) that created it.
- He opens us to the possibility that the being and inwardness of nature, not content with being merely looked at, will sometimes cast its loving eyes on us, and speak to us through its gestures.
- He goes beyond the religious and aesthetic appreciation of such things, implying that with this knowledge comes responsibility. Through our emancipation from nature we have indeed become co-creators with forces at our disposal, but should be on our guard against putting them to 'impious use'.

Co-creators? When a scientist uses the doctrine of our Divine Likeness to justify the cloning of human beings, I begin to question this. Does the agro-business have the right to terminate for profit the fertility of the grain in which Christ (the Word) so often named himself? I would call it blasphemy. And yet, it is the great pain and privilege of being human that we re-create the outer world in the image of our utterance. If something 'impious' still clings to that image then, naturally, we must suffer whatever consequence the world gives back to us.

## *Re-cognising*

Already in his time Nerval recognised the urgent need for such a change of consciousness, but (like the Romantic poets before him) he left it to others to elaborate a path to facilitate that change. I have (with the help of Rudolf Steiner's work) tried to pursue this through a series of exercises and permissions of language designed to encourage a faculty of imagination capable of apprehending 'the inside of the world and the outside of the mind'. Let the green heart of the Ashdown Forest be the emblem of it (see p.11).

The practices basic to this path are:

* Being willing to play and be silly.
* Giving devoted attention to the things, plants, animals and people that we encounter.
* Employing the qualitative language of Earth, Water, Air and Fire as a bridge between inner and outer experience.
* Regarding outer phenomena as the physiognomy through which the soul of the earth expresses its inwardness.
* Observing the difference between things, and how our feelings change in response to them (becoming cognisant thereby of the qualities of the world).
* Exercising the seemingly paradoxical faculty of 'exact sensory imagination'.
* Being awake in your sleep/asleep in your waking.

The practice of between-ness, is what I call it – a theme which is woven fine into the many 'spells' that bind this book together. I seek, through them, to engage your 'inter-est', shifting focus away from the finished things of our existence, and giving attention to the subtleties that eddy in the gaps between. I call them interludes; momentary playgrounds; silly, soul-y, holy places; points of jeopardy.

Some of these playgrounds nature herself provides. Springtime is surely one of them – a place/time when image and colour (hidden all winter long) are, momentarily, manifest. Sunset over the Medway valley – that is another (I keep thinking that the word *Medway* itself holds something of that in-between mercurial quality). Others encountered by us along the way have been created artfully out of somebody's appreciation of such thresholds – the Ha-Ha where cultivated garden gives way to wilderness; the Flow Forms where fixed and fluid meet in rhythmic play; the St. John memorial garden where moles and meditants busy themselves among the ashes of the dead. No doubt you can find such places in your own vicinity. It might be where two words meet, simple as that, or in a gasp of recognition between one breath and the next. In these vulnerable interludes between truth and lie, sleep and waking, or on the magic tide line between sea and sand (see p.231) the world soul scribes her joys and sufferings, and we (out of the corner of our eye) can decipher her alphabet.

## Re-viewing

After this general gathering of themes we called to mind our more personal memories and responses – the changing weather that accompanied us, the dry carrot cake served to us in the tea shop, the bird that kept tapping at our window as we studied the 'Ode to a Nightingale'. This more intimate stage of the review could include a consideration of *how* you worked together, and questions that possibly remain unanswered. Again, after warming to the task orally, the social writing techniques that we had developed together proved to be the best means of taking it further:

X 104. **Write, with a partner, such memories of the group's time together, naming things that happened, people you encountered, fine lines that were written, things you thought but didn't say. Don't forget to include** appreciations of each other. You could have two papers going back and forth between you; and if you again employ those repeated phrases, *I remember*, or *Do you remember?*, or *I'll never forget*, you will be able to gather many random impressions into a coherent piece of writing.

## Enter-taining

This looking back, besides serving the assimilation process, warmed us to our final task of 'entertaining' the wider community through the work we had done. I like that word. Its original meaning is *to hold together*, and in that spirit we filled the rafters of our hut with helium balloons and hung words from the dangling strings... 'matter...' 'pattern...' 'soul...' phrases that had been important to us... 'even stones have a love...' Every now and then during the presentation of our poems and stories we asked someone in the audience to pull on one of the threads and read out what was written there... 'God make gardners better nomenclators...' And when our programme was over we took those balloons outside and ceremoniously released them. We giggled a little as we watched them rising over the trees, because they looked like the sperm you sometimes see on television, wriggling their way towards some glorious multicoloured consummation. Now that the giggling has subsided, however, the image seems rather apt considering that our very first writing task (see p.27) was to write one word as a 'seed' for our work together. So, there we were, broadcasting many seed words and phrases... 'The poet is responsible for the animals...' out over Tablehurst Farm, across the River Medway, the Ashdown Forest... 'wind will shake each leaf type its own true way...' into a world hungry for poetry... 'the sower soweth the Word...' as grain to multiply, some sixtyfold, some a hundredfold. I trust they have floated down by now into the hands of those who need them.

## Words in place

The next day we followed the example of those balloons and set off over the horizon to visit the 'Seven Sisters', the high chalk cliffs near Eastbourne that our black and white flint stone (see p.61) had once been part of. As we were driving along the country roads towards the South Downs I remembered a local story of how Adam, upon being thrown out of paradise, went searching for the next best place to live. So enchanted he was with the county of Sussex that in order not to forget it as he travelled onwards he did a topsy-turvy naming of it, calling the ups the 'Downs' and  the downs the ups, the village of Lower Beeding being at the top of a hill while Upper Beeding is at the bottom of one. I don't know of any story, however, which fully explains how, near the village of Wilmington, the gleaming figure of the 'Long Man' came to be carved into the hillside:

Long Man of Wilmington

This figure, the largest image of the human being in Europe, is outlined in chalk. He is (now I think of it) all our four realms of nature gathered in one – grass growing within his stony lineaments, the white sheep grazing his edges as he holds open some gate to imagination, over the Seven Hills, to Faeryland. We stood there gazing for a while, then drove on past him down to Cuckmere Haven. No more herding of animals into our narrow pens – it was sheer delight to be out with them, sheep, and crows and cows, a tree shaped like a cow, the shadows of the seagulls moving against the white cliff face, the sea wind unbunging our ears.

We spent quite a while in silence, scouring the beach for treasures. Somebody had graciously scattered some plastic bottles all over the place, so before we left for home we set them up for targets and, with the stones provided, brought our throwing skills to a final perfection.

Whatever we lose (like a you or a me)
it's always ourselves we find in the sea[2]

is what e.e. cummings would have said if he had been there, but he wasn't, and so (teacher to the last) I muttered it for him. Here are some lines that I wrote:

Between the salt sea and the sea sand
there's an acre of land, so the old song says,
and a True Love waiting for the one who finds it.

That's a lie, Song, I say. Here's feathers and oil.
Here's an old shoe lolling its tongue,
but no sign anywhere of that magic acre.

Say what you please, but it's the truth I sing.
Every seventh wave brings Venus on her sea-borne shell.
What's the tongue lolling for but its loss of magic?

*PM*

The Seven Sisters

X 105. In the end, perhaps, all our work comes to this – to sit down in a place and, focusing our attention through the narrow nib of a pen, spell out what moves there in the moment.

If you sit down at the 'Seven Sisters' you are sure to get chalk on your bottom.

## St. John's Fire

Later, upon our return to the College, we celebrated the St. John's festival with the whole community, finishing the evening with a large bonfire. Maybe you remember the verse by Francis Edmunds that I quoted when we first took Fire as the focus for our attention (see p.86). He originally wrote it to help us participate meaningfully in this neglected festival. Here are its two subsequent stanzas ('to be spoken when the fire is at its height'):

> May the fire of love
> Consuming the dead wood within our souls
> Unite us with the living word of John:
> 'He must increase but I must decrease.'

> So may the mingling of the many flames
> Betoken the interweaving of our destinies
> In sacrificial deeds of love
> To lift a beacon of new hope for all.[3]

John the Baptist originally spoke those words regarding his relationship to the Christ,[4] and it is not by chance that they are uttered again at this time of the year when, having reached the solstice, the light begins its slow decline into winter. On a more personal level they become real for me when, seeing the light of

the bonfire flickering on the faces of those who have worked with me, I know I must relinquish any notion of knowledge or fame that I might cling to, and let theirs shine.

## *Larks and nightingales*

Here, at his most poetic, is Rudolf Steiner speaking of the relationship of language to the world:

> Mankind has long ago forgotten why the songbirds sing. It is
> true that men have preserved the art of song, the art of poetry,

233

but in the age of intellectualism in which the intellect has dominated everything, they have forgotten the connection of singing with the whole universe... For when at a certain time of year the larks and the nightingales sing, what is thereby formed streams out into the cosmos, not through the air, but through the ethereal element; it vibrates outward in the cosmos up to a certain boundary... then it vibrates back again to earth, to be received by the animal realm – only now the divine-spiritual essence of the cosmos has united with it... In those ancient times this was understood, and therefore the pupils of the Mystery schools were instructed in such singing and dancing as they could then perform at the St. John's festival, if I may call it by the modern name. Human beings sent this out into the cosmos, of course not now in animal form, but in humanised form, as a further development of what the animals send out into cosmic space. And there is something else yet that belonged to those festivals: not only the dancing, the music, the song, but afterward, the listening. First there was the active performance in the festivals; then the people were directed to listen to what came back to them. For through their dances, their singing, and all that was poetic in their performances, they had sent forth the great questions to the divine spiritual of the cosmos.[5]

## Twelve windows

On our very last morning we gathered in our 'hut' which we had filled with so many words and imaginations. We spent some time taking our pictures off the walls – the flint stones we had drawn, the plants, the animals sketched with our eyes shut, the river Alph plunging down into 'the caverns measureless to man'. Even Botticelli's *Primavera* was gone. We swept the floor and mopped it; emptied the candle-holder of its burnt matches; polished the bronze dog on the piano. Then finally we sat down together to say where we were going after this and whether we would ever again put pen to paper. The room looked strangely bare. Its two doors. Its seven rafters. Its twelve windows. A very humble wooden hut and yet, in its numbering, close to fairy tale, and open to the cosmos.

I closed our time together by speaking some words of mine inspired by that place:

> Here we are
> in a room
> with twelve windows.
>
> As we listen
> we are looked at
>
> by the twelve disciples
> by the twelve
> signs of the Zodiac
>
> This is a lie
> but I believe it.
>
> Please believe it too
> or the room
> shrinks to a size
> that won't contain us.

*PM*

With that in mind we joined hands and, with a swing, sent the circle we had formed up through the rafters into the wide sky, trusting it would link with other creative circles known and unknown to us.

## *Notes*

1. de Nerval, G., *Bending the Bow*, trans. by Duncan, R., New Directions Publishing Corporation, 1968, p.92
2. cummings, e.e., *Selected Poems*, Penguin Books, 1960
3. Edmunds, L.F., *Circles*, Emerson College, 1990
4. *The Holy Bible*, The Gospel According to St. John, Authorised Version, Ch.3, verses 30
5. Steiner, R., *The Cycle of the Year*, Anthroposophic Press, 1984, p.58

# Postscript

Here, gathered into a rather tight nutshell, are my thoughts on the dynamics of the creative polarities we have been working with:

**INNER WORLD**
(subjective)
Word

**OUTER WORLD**
(objective)
Image

We can recall here what Basho said:

**The trouble with most poetry is that it is either subjective or objective.**[1]

And we can add to it a further polarisation, drawn from the American poet Wendell Berry's perception (see p.5) that there are two diseases of language which need to be healed through our finding of a middle ground:[2]

**Language in which the speaker is present but the world is absent**

**Language in which the world is present but the speaker is absent**

That middle ground where (according to Berry) we 'stand by our words' is surely the place of action for those faculties that we have been exercising throughout these pages:

**Observing**

**Thinking**

**Remembering**

**Imagining**

At this turning point their collaborative activity can bring inner and outer worlds into creative relationship:

| | |
|---|---|
| **The inner world seeks utterance (through image)** | **The outer world seeks innerance (through word)** |

Or, as the Imagist poet William Carlos Williams put it:

**No ideas but in things**[3]   To which I would add:   **No things but in ideas**

Jacob Boehme said it this way:   The necessary corollary of which is:

**Whatever the self describes describes the Self**[4]   **Whatever describes the soul is itself ensouled**

I say it this way:

**If we lend the world our subjectivity   the world will lend us its objectivity**

In literary terms we speak about the power of metaphor to 'carry across' the gap between inner and outer. The following verse by Rudolf Steiner, however, lifts it to another level:

> **Through the wide world there lives and moves**
> **The real being of Man,**
> **While in the innermost core of Man**
> **The mirror-image of the world is living.**
>
> **The I unites the two,**
> **And thus fulfils**
> **The meaning of existence.**[5]

## Notes

[1]  Basho, M., source not traced
[2]  Berry, W., *Standing by Words*, North Point Press, 1983, p.24
[3]  Williams, W.C., *A Sort of Song*, 1944
[4]  Boehme, J., source not traced
[5]  Steiner, R., *Verses and Meditations*, Rudolf Steiner Press, 1979, p.59

# Appendix: Little Snow White

Once upon a time in the middle of winter, when the flakes of snow were falling like feathers from the sky, a queen sat at a window sewing, and the frame of the window was made of black ebony. And whilst she was sewing and looking out of the window at the snow, she pricked her finger with the needle, and three drops of blood fell upon the snow. And the red looked pretty upon the white snow, and she thought to herself, 'Would that I had a child as white as snow, as red as blood, and as black as the wood of the window-frame.' Soon after that she had a little daughter, who was as white as snow, and as red as blood, and her hair was as black as ebony; and she was therefore called Little Snow White. And when the child was born, the Queen died.

After a year had passed the King took to himself another wife. She was a beautiful woman, but proud and haughty, and she could not bear that anyone else should surpass her in beauty. She had a wonderful looking-glass, and when she stood in front of it and looked at herself in it, and said –

> 'Looking-glass, Looking-glass, on the wall,
> Who in this land is the fairest of all?'

The looking-glass answered –

> 'Thou, O Queen, art the fairest of all!'

240

Then she was satisfied, for she knew that the looking-glass spoke the truth.

But Snow White was growing up, and grew more and more beautiful; and when she was seven years old she was as beautiful as the day, and more beautiful than the Queen herself. And once when the Queen asked her looking-glass –

'Looking-glass, Looking-glass, on the wall,
Who in this land is the fairest of all?'

it answered –

'Thou art fairer than all who are here, Lady Queen.'
But more beautiful still is Snow White, as I ween.'

Then the Queen was shocked, and turned yellow and green with envy. From that hour, whenever she looked at Snow White, her heart heaved in her breast, she hated the girl so much. And envy and pride grew higher and higher in her heart like a weed, so that she had no peace day or night. She called a huntsman, and said, 'Take the child away into the forest; I will no longer have her in my sight. Kill her, and bring me back her heart as a token.' The huntsman obeyed, and took her away; but when he had drawn his knife, and was about to pierce Snow White's innocent heart, she began to weep, and said, 'Ah dear huntsman, leave me my life! I will run away into the wild forest, and never come home again.' And as she was so beautiful the huntsman had pity on her and said, 'Run away, then, you poor child.' 'The wild beasts will soon have devoured you,' thought he, and yet it seemed as if a stone had been rolled from his heart since it was no longer needful for him to kill her. And as a young boar just then came running by he stabbed it, and cut out its heart and took it to the Queen as proof that the child was dead. The cook had to salt this, and the wicked Queen ate it, and thought she had eaten the heart of Snow White.

But now the poor child was all alone in the great forest, and so terrified that she looked at every leaf of every tree, and did not know what to do. Then she began to run, and ran over sharp stones and through thorns, and the wild beasts ran past her, but did her no harm. She ran as long as her feet would go until it was almost evening; then she saw a little cottage and went into it to rest herself. Everything in the cottage was small, but neater and cleaner than can be told. There was a table on which was a white cover, and seven little plates, and on each plate a little spoon; moreover, there were seven little knives and forks, and seven little mugs. Against the wall stood seven little beds side by side, and covered with snow-white counterpanes. Little Snow White was so hungry and thirsty that she ate some vegetables and bread from each plate and drank a drop of wine out of each mug, for she did not wish to take all from one only. Then, as she was so tired, she laid herself down on one of the little beds, but none of them suited her; one was too long, another too short, but at last she found that the seventh one was right, and so she remained in it, said a prayer and went to sleep.

When it was quite dark the owners of the cottage came back; they were seven dwarfs who dug and delved in the mountains for ore. They lit their seven candles, and as it was now light within the cottage they saw that someone had been there, for everything was not in the same order in which they had left it.

The first said, 'Who has been sitting on my chair?'
The second, 'Who has been eating off my plate?'
The third, 'Who has been taking some of my bread?'
The fourth, 'Who has been eating my vegetables?'
The fifth, 'Who has been using my fork?'
The sixth, 'Who has been cutting with my knife?'
The seventh, 'Who has been drinking out of my mug?'

242

Then the first looked round and saw that there was a little hole on his bed, and he said, 'Who has been getting into my bed?' The others came up and each called out, 'Somebody has been lying in my bed too.' But the seventh when he looked at his bed saw little Snow White, who was lying asleep therein. And he called the others, who came running up, and they cried out with astonishment, and brought their seven little candles and let the light fall on little Snow White. 'Oh, heavens! oh, heavens!' cried they, 'what a lovely child!' and they were so glad that they did not wake her up, but let her sleep on in the bed. And the seventh dwarf slept with his companions, one hour with each, and so got through the night.

When it was morning little Snow White awoke, and was frightened when she saw the seven dwarfs. But they were friendly and asked her what her name was. 'My name is Snow White,' she answered. 'How have you come to our house?' said the dwarfs. Then she told them that her step-mother had wished to have her killed, but that the huntsman had spared her life, and that she had run for the whole day, until at last she had found their dwelling. The dwarfs said, 'If you will take care of our house, cook, make the beds, wash, sew, and knit, and if you will keep everything neat and clean, you can stay with us and you shall want for nothing.' 'Yes,' said Snow White, 'with all my heart,' and she stayed with them. She kept the house in order for them; in the mornings they went to the mountains and looked for copper and gold, in the evenings they came back, and then their supper had to be ready. The girl was alone the whole day, so the good dwarfs warned her and said, 'Beware of your step-mother, she will soon know that you are here; be sure to let no one come in.'

But the Queen, believing that she had eaten Snow White's heart, could not but think that she was again the first and most beautiful of all; and she went to her looking-glass and said –

> 'Looking-glass, Looking-glass, on the wall,
> Who in this land is the fairest of all?'

and the glass answered –

> 'Oh, Queen, thou art fairest of all I see,
> But over the hills, where the seven dwarfs dwell,
> Snow White is still alive and well,
> And none is so fair as she.'

Then she was astounded, for she knew that the looking-glass never spoke falsely, and she knew that the huntsman had betrayed her, and that little Snow White was still alive.

And so she thought and thought again how she might kill her, for so long as she was not the fairest in the whole land, envy let her have no rest. And when she had at last thought of something to do, she painted her face, and dressed herself like an old peddler-woman, and no one could have known her. In this disguise she went over the seven mountains to the seven dwarfs, and knocked at the door and cried, 'Pretty things to sell, very cheap, very cheap.' Little Snow White looked out of the window and called out, 'Good-day my good woman, what have you to sell?' 'Good things, pretty things,' she answered; 'stay-laces of all colours,' and she pulled out one which was woven of bright-coloured silk. 'I may let the worthy old woman in,' thought Snow White, and she unbolted the door and bought the pretty laces. 'Child,' said the old woman, 'what a fright you look; come, I will lace you properly for once.' Snow White had no suspicion, but stood before her, and let herself be laced with the new laces. But the old woman laced so quickly and so tightly that Snow White lost her breath and fell down as if dead. 'Now I am the most beautiful,' said the Queen to herself, and ran away.

Not long afterwards, in the evening, the seven dwarfs came

home, but how shocked they were when they saw their dear little Snow White lying on the ground, and that she neither stirred nor moved, and seemed to be dead. They lifted her up, and, as they saw that she was laced too tightly, they cut the laces; then she began to breathe a little, and after a while came to life again. When the dwarfs heard what had happened they said, 'The old peddler-woman was no one else than the wicked Queen; take care and let no one come in when we are not with you.'

But the wicked woman when she had reached home went in front of the glass and asked –

'Looking-glass, Looking-glass, on the wall,
Who in this land is the fairest of all?'

and it answered as before –

'Oh, Queen, thou art fairest of all I see,
But over the hills, where the seven dwarfs dwell,
Snow White is still alive and well,
And none is so fair as she.'

When she heard that, all her blood rushed to her heart with fear, for she saw plainly that little Snow White was again alive. 'But now,' she said, 'I will think of something that shall put an end to you,' and by the help of witchcraft, which she understood, she made a poisonous comb. Then she disguised herself and took the shape of another old woman. So she went over the seven mountains to the seven dwarfs, knocked at the door, and cried, 'Good things to sell, cheap, cheap!' Little Snow White looked out and said, 'Go away; I cannot let any one come in.' 'I suppose you can look,' said the old woman, and pulled the poisonous comb out and held it up. It pleased the girl so well that she let herself be beguiled, and opened the door. When they had made a bargain the old woman said, 'Now I will comb you properly for once.' Poor little Snow White had no suspicion, and let the old woman do as she pleased, but hardly had she put the comb in her hair than the poison in it took effect, and the girl fell down senseless. 'You paragon of beauty,' said the wicked woman, 'you are done for now,' and she went away.

But fortunately it was almost evening, when the seven dwarfs came home. When they saw Snow White lying as if dead upon the ground they at once suspected the step-mother, and they looked and found the poisoned comb. Scarcely had they taken it out when Snow White came to herself, and told them what had happened. Then they warned her once more to be upon her guard and to open the door to no one.

The Queen, at home, went in front of the glass and said –

> 'Looking-glass, Looking-glass, on the wall,
> Who in this land is the fairest of all?'

then it answered as before –

> 'Oh, Queen, thou art fairest of all I see,
> But over the hills, where the seven dwarfs dwell,
> Snow White is still alive and well,
> And none is so fair as she.'

When she heard the glass speak thus she trembled and shook with rage. 'Snow White shall die,' she cried, 'even if it costs me my life!'

Thereupon she went into a quite secret, lonely room, where no one ever came, and there she made a very poisonous apple. Outside it looked pretty, white with a red cheek, so that everyone who saw it longed for it; but whoever ate a piece of it must surely die.

When the apple was ready she painted her face, and dressed

herself up as a country-woman, and so she went over the seven mountains to the seven dwarfs. She knocked at the door. Snow White put her head out of the window and said, 'I cannot let any one in; the seven dwarfs have forbidden me.' 'It is all the same to me,' answered the woman, 'I shall soon get rid of my apples. There, I will give you one.'

'No,' said Snow White, 'I dare not take anything.' 'Are you afraid of poison?' said the old woman; 'look, I will cut the apple in two pieces; you eat the red cheek, and I will eat the white.' The apple was so cunningly made that only the red cheek was poisoned. Snow White longed for the fine apple, and when she saw that the woman ate part of it she could resist no longer, and stretched out her hand and took the poisonous half. But hardly had she a bit of it in her mouth than she fell down dead. Then the Queen looked at her with a dreadful look, and laughed aloud and said, 'White as snow, red as blood, black as ebony-wood! This time the dwarfs cannot wake you up again.'

And when she asked of the Looking-glass at home –

'Looking-glass, Looking-glass, on the wall,
Who in this land is the fairest of all?'

it answered at last –

'Oh, Queen, in this land thou art fairest of all.'

Then her envious heart had rest, so far as an envious heart can have rest.

The dwarfs, when they came home in the evening, found Snow White lying upon the ground; she breathed no longer and was dead. They lifted her up, looked to see whether they could find anything poisonous, unlaced her, combed her hair, washed her with water and wine, but it was all of no use; the poor child was dead, and remained dead. They laid her upon a bier, and all seven of them sat round it and wept for her, and wept three days long. Then they were going to bury her, but she still looked as if she were living, and still had her pretty red cheeks. They said, 'We could not bury her in the dark ground,' and they had a transparent coffin of glass made, so that she could be seen from all sides, and they laid her in it, and wrote her name upon it in golden letters, and that she was a king's daughter. Then they put the coffin out upon the mountain, and one of them always stayed by it and watched it. And birds came too, and wept for Snow White; first an owl, then a raven, and last a dove. And now Snow White lay a long, long time in the coffin, and she did not change, but looked as if she were asleep; for she was as white as snow, as red as blood, and her hair was as black as ebony.

It happened, however, that a king's son came into the forest, and went to the dwarfs' house to spend the night. He saw the coffin on the mountain, and the beautiful Snow White within it, and read what was written upon it in golden letters. Then he said to the dwarfs, 'Let me have the coffin, I will give you whatever you want for it.' But the dwarfs answered, 'We will not part with it for all the gold in the world.' Then he said, 'Let me have it as a gift, for I cannot live without seeing Snow White. I will honour and prize her as my dearest possession.' As he spoke in this way the good dwarfs took pity upon him, and gave him the coffin.

And now the King's son had it carried away by his servants on their shoulders. And it happened that they stumbled over a tree-stump, and with the shock the poisonous piece of apple which Snow White had bitten off came out of her throat. And before long she opened her eyes, lifted up the lid of the coffin, sat up, and was once more alive. 'Oh, heavens, where am I?' she cried. The King's son, full of joy, said, 'You are with me,' and told her what had happened, and said, 'I love you more than everything in the world; come with me to my father's palace, you shall be my wife.'

And Snow White was willing, and went with him, and their wedding was held with great show and splendour. But Snow White's wicked step-mother was also bidden to the feast. When she had arrayed herself in beautiful clothes she went before the Looking-glass, and said –

'Looking-glass, Looking-glass, on the wall,
Who in this land is the fairest of all?'

the glass answered –

'Oh, Queen, of all here the fairest art thou,
But the young Queen is fairer by far as I trow.'

Then the wicked woman uttered a curse, and was so wretched, so utterly wretched, that she knew not what to do. At first she would not go to the wedding at all, but she had no peace, and must go to see the young Queen. And when she went in she knew Snow White; and she stood still with rage and fear, and could not stir. But iron slippers had already been put upon the fire, and they were brought in with tongs, and set before her. Then she was forced to put on the red-hot shoes, and dance until she dropped down dead.

*From Jacob and Wilhelm Grimm,* Household Tales, *trans. Margaret Hunt, London, George Bell, 1884, based on the last revised version of the Grimm's tales.*

# Bibliography

Abbs, P., (ed) *Earth Songs*, Green Books, 2002

Abrams, A., *The Spell of the Sensuous*, Panteon Books, 1996

Barfield, O., *Poetic Diction*, Faber and Faber, 1973

Barfield, O., *Romanticism Comes of Age*, Rudolf Steiner Press, 1966

Barfield, O., *Saving the Appearances*, Faber and Faber, 1957

Barfield, O., *Speakers' Meaning*, Rudolf Steiner Press, 1967

Bate, J., *The Song of the Earth*, Picador, 2000

Berry, W., *Standing by Words*, North Point Press, 1983

Colquhoun, M., and Ewald, A., *New Eyes for Plants*, Hawthorn Press, 1996

Davy, J., *Hope, Evolution and Change*, Hawthorn Press, 1985

Duncan, R., *The Truth and Life of Myth*, The Sumac Press, 1968

Goldberg, N., *Writing Down the Bones*, Shambala, 1986

Holdredge, C., *The Flexible Giant*, The Nature Institute, 2003

Lehrs, E., *Man or Matter*, Faber and Faber, 1958

Penn, R., *Portrait of Ashdown Forest*, Robert Hale, 1984

Raine, K., *Defending Ancient Springs – 'On the Mythological'*, Oxford University Press, 1967

Rothenberg, J., (ed) *Technicians of the Sacred*, Anchor Books, 1969

Schad, W., *Man and Mammals*, Waldorf Press, 1977

Steiner, R., *Man as Symphony of the Creative Word*, Rudolf Steiner Press, 1978

Wilkes, J., *Flow Forms*, Floris Books, 2003

Willard, B., *The Forest*, Sweethaws Press, 1989

Yeats, W. B., *A Vision*, Collier Books, 1966

# Index

Paul Matthews is available to give workshops and poetry readings. Please contact him at paul.matthews@emerson.org.uk    Details of his other courses, including the Poetry OtherWise summer school, can be found at www.emerson.org.uk

# Other books by Hawthorn Press

## Sing Me the Creation

PAUL MATTHEWS

This is an inspirational workbook of creative writing exercises for poets and teachers, and for all who wish to develop the life of the imagination. There are over 300 exercises for improving writing skills. Though intended for group work with adults, teachers will find these exercises easily adaptable to the classroom.

Paul Matthews, a poet himself, taught creative writing at Emerson College, Sussex.

**224pp; 214 x 135mm; 978-1-869890-60-5; pb**

## The Winding Road

Family treasury of poems and verses

COMPILED BY MATTHEW BARTON

Celebrate each age and stage of your child's life with this poetic travelling companion. The Winding Road offers over 200 poems on the theme of childhood and growing up by writers ancient and modern — from Gaelic blessings to Navajo prayers, from William Blake to Eleanor Farjeon and Billy Collins.

This rich treasury of poems, verses, blessings and meditations reflects a child's journey from baby to teenager, from first milestones to leaving home:-

Matthew Barton is a translator, editor, teacher and poet. He also taught kindergarten for many years at the Bristol Waldorf School.

**224pp; 210 x 148mm; 978-1-903458-47-1; pb**

# Getting in touch with Hawthorn Press

**What are your pressing questions about the early years?**
The Hawthorn Early Years Series arises from parents' and educators' pressing questions and concerns – so please contact us with your questions. These will help spark new books, workshops or festivals if there is sufficient interest. We will be delighted to hear your views on our Early Years books, how they can be improved, and what your needs are.

Visit our website for details of the Early Years Series and forthcoming books and events:

http://www.hawthornpress.com

# Ordering books

If you have difficulties ordering Hawthorn Press books from a bookshop, you can order direct from:

**United Kingdom**
> Booksource
> 50 Cambuslang Road, Cambuslang, Glasgow
> G32 8NB
> Tel: 0845 370 0063
> Fax: 0845 370 0064
> E-mail: orders@booksource.net

**USA/North America**
> Steiner Books
> PO Box 960, Herndon
> VA 20172-0960
> Tel: (800) 856 8664
> Fax: (703) 661 1501
> E-mail: service@steinerbooks.org